Easy Recipes For Peas And Beans

Leanna .X Kouma

All rights reserved. Copyright © 2024 Leanna .X Kouma

COPYRIGHT © 2024 Leanna .X Kouma

All rights reserved.

No part of this book must be reproduced, stored in a retrieval system, or shared by any means, electronic, mechanical, photocopying, recording, or otherwise, without written permission from the publisher.

Every precaution has been taken in the preparation of this book; still the publisher and author assume no responsibility for errors or omissions. Nor do they assume any liability for damages resulting from the use of the information contained herein.

Legal Notice:

This book is copyright protected and is only meant for your individual use. You are not allowed to amend, distribute, sell, use, quote or paraphrase any of its part without the written consent of the author or publisher.

Introduction

This book cookbook is a treasure trove of culinary delights centered around the versatile and nutritious ingredients of beans and peas. With a vast array of recipes spanning various types of beans and peas, this cookbook offers something to suit every palate and occasion.

Starting with black beans, the cookbook presents a diverse range of recipes that showcase the rich and hearty flavors of this popular legume. From classic black bean soup to zesty black bean salads and flavorful bean burgers, there are endless possibilities for incorporating black beans into your culinary repertoire.

Moving on to black-eyed beans, the cookbook continues to delight with innovative and mouthwatering recipes that highlight the unique taste and texture of this legume. From traditional Southern-style black-eyed pea stew to vibrant salads and satisfying bean dips, there's no shortage of ways to enjoy the wholesome goodness of black-eyed beans.

For those looking to explore the culinary potential of fava beans, the cookbook offers a tantalizing selection of recipes that capture the essence of this beloved legume. From hearty fava bean soups and stews to refreshing salads and savory fava bean spreads, each recipe celebrates the earthy flavor and nutritional benefits of fava beans in its own unique way.

Whether you're a seasoned bean enthusiast or just beginning to explore the world of legume-based cooking, this cookbook provides endless inspiration and guidance for creating delicious meals year-round. With its diverse range of recipes, clear instructions, and helpful tips, it invites readers to embark on a flavorful journey through the wonderful world of beans and peas.

Contents

Chapter 1: Black Beans 1
1. Air Fryer Egg Rolls 2
   Ingredients 2
   Direction 3
   Nutrition Information 3
2. Alligator Chili 4
   Ingredients 4
   Direction 5
   Nutrition Information 5
3. Baja Salad 6
   Ingredients 6
   Direction 7
   Nutrition Information 7
4. Baked Chimichangas with Nopales and Poblano 8
   Ingredients 8
   Direction 8
   Nutrition Information 9
5. Balela Chickpea and Black Bean Salad 10
   Ingredients 10
   Direction 10
   Nutrition Information 11
6. Beef Enchiladas with Homemade Sauce 12
   Ingredients 12
   Direction 12
   Nutrition Information 13
7. Beef Taco Noodle Casserole 14
   Ingredients 14
   Direction 14
   Nutrition Information 15
8. Best Bean Salad 16

Ingredients 16
Direction 16
Nutrition Information 17
9. Best Beef Enchiladas 18
Ingredients 18
Direction 18
Nutrition Information 19
10. Best Black Beans 20
Ingredients 20
Direction 20
Nutrition Information 20
11. Black Bean and CornQuesadillas 21
Ingredients 21
Direction 21
Nutrition Information 22
12. Black Bean and Corn Salsafrom RED GOLD 23
Ingredients 23
Direction 23
Nutrition Information 23
13. Black Bean and CornVegetarian Burger 25
Ingredients 25
Direction 25
Nutrition Information 26
14. Black Bean and Potato VeggieBurgers 27
Ingredients 27
Direction 27
Nutrition Information 28
15. Black Bean and White CornSalad 29
Ingredients 29
Direction 29
Nutrition Information 29
16. Black Bean Breakfast Bowl 31
Ingredients 31

Direction 31
Nutrition Information 31
17.   Black Bean Cigars 33
Ingredients 33
Direction 33
Nutrition Information 34
18.   Black Bean Corn and TomatoSalad with Feta Cheese 35
Ingredients 35
Direction 35
Nutrition Information 36
19.   Black Bean Quinoa Burgers 37
Ingredients 37
Direction 37
Nutrition Information 38
20.   Black Bean Salsa Soup 39
Ingredients 39
Direction 39
Nutrition Information 40
21.   Black Bean Soup with Riceand Sherry 41
Ingredients 41
Direction 41
Nutrition Information 42
22.   Black Bean Stuffed Peppers 43
Ingredients 43
Direction 43
Nutrition Information 44
23.   Black Beans and Pork Chops 45
Ingredients 45
Direction 45
Nutrition Information 45
24.   Bulgur Chili 47
Ingredients 47
Direction 47

Nutrition Information 48
25. Candices Butternut SquashEnchiladas 49
Ingredients 49
Direction 49
Nutrition Information 50
26. Caribbean Wrap 51
Ingredients 51
Direction 51
Nutrition Information 51
27. Chicken and Black Bean Chili 53
Ingredients 53
Direction 53
Nutrition Information 54
28. Chicken and Two Bean Chili 55
Ingredients 55
Direction 55
Nutrition Information 56
29. Chicken Nachos fromReynolds Wrap 57
Ingredients 57
Direction 57
Nutrition Information 58
30. Chicken Tortilla Soup IV 59
Ingredients 59
Direction 59
Nutrition Information 60
31. Coconut Rice with BlackBeans 61
Ingredients 61
Direction 61
Nutrition Information 61
32. Corned Beef Hash BreakfastTacos 63
Ingredients 63
Direction 63
Nutrition Information 64

33. Cottage Cheese Avocado andBlack Bean Salsa 65
Ingredients 65
Direction 65
Nutrition Information 66
34. Double Crust Bean Pie 67
Ingredients 67
Direction 67
Nutrition Information 68
35. Easy Black Beans and Rice 69
Ingredients 69
Direction 69
36. Easy Black Beans andTomatoes 70
Ingredients 70
Direction 70
Nutrition Information 70
37. Easy Chicken Fajita Soup 71
Ingredients 71
Direction 71
Nutrition Information 72
38. Easy Turkey Chili 73
Ingredients 73
Direction 73
Nutrition Information 74
39. Enchilada Casserole 75
Ingredients 75
Direction 75
Nutrition Information 76
40. Fiesta Chicken and Black Bean Enchiladas from Mission 77
Ingredients 77
Direction 77
Nutrition Information 78
41. Flaming Burritos 79
Ingredients 79

Direction	79
Nutrition Information	80
42. Goya Black Bean Salsa	81
Ingredients	81
Direction	81
43. Grillable Vegan Burger	82
Ingredients	82
Direction	82
Nutrition Information	83
44. Hash Brown Tostadas	84
Ingredients	84
Direction	84
Nutrition Information	85
45. Hearty Ham Bone Black BeanSoup	86
Ingredients	86
Direction	86
Nutrition Information	87
46. Herbed Rice and Spicy BlackBean Salad	88
Ingredients	88
Direction	88
Nutrition Information	89
47. Hispanic Tilapia and RiceBowl	90
Ingredients	90
Direction	90
Nutrition Information	91
48. Instant Pot Vegan 15BeanSoup	92
Ingredients	92
Direction	92
Nutrition Information	93
49. Jennifers Corn Salad	94
Ingredients	94
Direction	94
Nutrition Information	94

50. Kellys Black Bean Salad	96
Ingredients	96
Direction	96
Nutrition Information	97
51. Leftover Salmon Lunch Wrap	98
Ingredients	98
Direction	98
Nutrition Information	98
52. LowCarb GlutenFree BlackBean and Lentil Burgers	100
Ingredients	100
Direction	100
Nutrition Information	101
53. Mexican Bean and Rice Salad	102
Ingredients	102
Direction	102
Nutrition Information	102
54. Mexican Casserole	104
Ingredients	104
Direction	104
Nutrition Information	105
55. Mexican Fiesta with SorghumGrain	106
Ingredients	106
Direction	106
Nutrition Information	107
56. Mexicorn	108
Ingredients	108
Direction	108
Nutrition Information	108
57. Old Mamas Fashioned Chili	109
Ingredients	109
Direction	109
Nutrition Information	110
58. Pacific Cuban Black Beansand Rice	111

Ingredients 111
Direction 112
Nutrition Information 112
59. PAMs Spicy Slow CookerChicken Tortilla Soup 113
Ingredients 113
Direction 113
Nutrition Information 114
60. Pumpkin Black Bean Soup 115
Ingredients 115
Direction 115
Nutrition Information 116
61. Quick and Easy EdamameSalad 117
Ingredients 117
Direction 117
Nutrition Information 117
62. Quick and Easy MexicanBreakfast Tacos 119
Ingredients 119
Direction 119
Nutrition Information 120
63. Quinoa and Black Bean Chili 121
Ingredients 121
Direction 121
Nutrition Information 122
64. Quinoa Bean and GroundTurkey Chili 123
Ingredients 123
Direction 123
Nutrition Information 124
65. Quinoa Black Bean Burgers 125
Ingredients 125
Direction 125
Nutrition Information 126
66. Race Day Salsa 127
Ingredients 127

Direction 127
Nutrition Information 128
67. Salmon Tacos 129
Ingredients 129
Direction 129
Nutrition Information 130
68. Sassy Spaghetti 131
Ingredients 131
Direction 131
Nutrition Information 131
69. Six Can Chicken Tortilla Soup 133
Ingredients 133
Direction 133
Nutrition Information 133
70. Slow Cooker ChickenEnchilada Soup 134
Ingredients 134
Direction 134
Nutrition Information 135
71. Slow Cooker Chicken TacoBowls 136
Ingredients 136
Direction 136
Nutrition Information 137
72. Smokey Vegetarian CubanBlack Bean Soup 138
Ingredients 138
Direction 139
Nutrition Information 139
73. Smoky Black Bean Burgers 140
Ingredients 140
Direction 140
Nutrition Information 140
74. Southwestern Egg Rolls withAvocado Cilantro Sauce 142
Ingredients 142
Direction 143

Nutrition Information 143
75.   Spicy Black and Red BeanSoup 144
Ingredients 144
Direction 144
Nutrition Information 145
76.   Spicy Three Bean Soup 146
Ingredients 146
Direction 146
Nutrition Information 147
77.   Spinach and Black Bean Pasta 148
Ingredients 148
Direction 148
Nutrition Information 149
78.   Stacked Fajita VegetableEnchilada Casserole 150
Ingredients 150
Direction 151
Nutrition Information 152
79.   Steel Mill Chili 153
Ingredients 153
Direction 153
Nutrition Information 153
80.   Stuffed Green Peppers 155
Ingredients 155
Direction 155
Nutrition Information 156
81.   Summer Salad with CuminCrusted Salmon 157
Ingredients 157
Direction 158
Nutrition Information 158
82.   Superfood Hummus 159
Ingredients 159
Direction 159
Nutrition Information 160

83. Taco Mix with Black Beans 161
   Ingredients 161
   Direction 161
   Nutrition Information 161
84. Tex Mex Black Bean Dip 163
   Ingredients 163
   Direction 163
   Nutrition Information 164
85. TexMex Turkey Chili withBlack Beans Corn and Butternut Squash 165
   Ingredients 165
   Direction 165
   Nutrition Information 166
86. The Best Turkey Chili 167
   Ingredients 167
   Direction 167
   Nutrition Information 168
87. ThreeBean Vegetarian Chili 169
   Ingredients 169
   Direction 169
   Nutrition Information 170
88. Val and Jesss Vegan AvocadoDip 171
   Ingredients 171
   Direction 171
   Nutrition Information 171
89. Vegan Black Bean and SweetPotato Salad 173
   Ingredients 173
   Direction 173
   Nutrition Information 174
90. Vegan Fajitas 175
   Ingredients 175
   Direction 175
   Nutrition Information 176
91. Vegan Sweet PotatoEnchiladas 177

Ingredients 177
Direction 177
Nutrition Information 178
92. Vegan Yuca Tacos 179
Ingredients 179
Direction 179
Nutrition Information 180
93. Vegetarian Black BeanBurritos 181
Ingredients 181
Direction 181
Nutrition Information 182
94. Veggie Pizzadillas 183
Ingredients 183
Direction 183
Nutrition Information 184
95. Zesty Quinoa Salad 185
Ingredients 185
Direction 185
Nutrition Information 186
   Chapter 2: Black-Eyed Beans 187
96. Avocado and Black Eyed PeaSalsa 188
Ingredients 188
Direction 188
Nutrition Information 188
97. Belas Stuffed Red BellPeppers 190
Ingredients 190
Direction 190
Nutrition Information 191
98. Best Ever Cowboy Caviar 192
Ingredients 192
Direction 192
Nutrition Information 193
99. Black Eyed Susan Salad 194

Ingredients 194
Direction 194
Nutrition Information 194
100. BlackEyed Pea BratwurstStew 196
Ingredients 196
Direction 196
Nutrition Information 197
101. BlackEyed Pea Gumbo 198
Ingredients 198
Direction 198
Nutrition Information 198
102. BlackEyed Pea Salad III 200
Ingredients 200
Direction 200
Nutrition Information 200
103. BlackEyed Pea Soup 201
Ingredients 201
Direction 201
Nutrition Information 202
104. BlackEyed Peas and Tortillas 203
Ingredients 203
Direction 203
Nutrition Information 203
105. BlackEyed Peas With CollardGreens and Turnips 205
Ingredients 205
Direction 205
Nutrition Information 206
106. Classic Texas Caviar 207
Ingredients 207
Direction 207
Nutrition Information 208
107. Cold BlackEyed Peas and Corn 209
Ingredients 209

Direction 209
Nutrition Information 209
108. Cold Corn Salsa 211
Ingredients 211
Direction 211
Nutrition Information 211
109. Cowboy Caviar 213
Ingredients 213
Direction 213
Nutrition Information 213
110. Deep Fried Black Eyed Peas 215
Ingredients 215
Direction 215
Nutrition Information 216
111. Delilahs Wicked Twelve AlarmChili 217
Ingredients 217
Direction 218
Nutrition Information 218
112. DownHome BlackEyed Peas 220
Ingredients 220
Direction 220
Nutrition Information 220
113. Easy Coconut Rice andBlackEyed Peas 222
Ingredients 222
Direction 222
Nutrition Information 222
114. Easy Hoppin John 223
Ingredients 223
Direction 223
Nutrition Information 223
115. Fabiennes BlackEyed CrabCakes 225
Ingredients 225
Direction 225

Nutrition Information 226
116. Fiesta Grilled Chicken 227
Ingredients 227
Direction 228
Nutrition Information 228
117. Fried BlackEye Peas 229
Ingredients 229
Direction 229
Nutrition Information 230
118. GlutenFree BlackEyed Pea andCauliflower Soup 231
Ingredients 231
Direction 231
Nutrition Information 232
119. Guyanese Cookup Rice 233
Ingredients 233
Direction 233
Nutrition Information 234
120. Hawg Wild BlackEyed Peas 235
Ingredients 235
Direction 236
Nutrition Information 236
121. Hearty Hoppin John Stew 237
Ingredients 237
Direction 237
Nutrition Information 238
122. Italian Hot Turkey Sausageand BlackEyed Peas 239
Ingredients 239
Direction 239
Nutrition Information 240
123. Kala BlackEyed Pea Frittersfrom the Dutch Antilles 241
Ingredients 241
Direction 241
Nutrition Information 242

124. Loaded Blackeyed Peas Spinach and Vegetable Soup 243
    Ingredients 243
    Direction 243
    Nutrition Information 244
125. Lucky Pea Soup 245
    Ingredients 245
    Direction 245
    Nutrition Information 246
126. Melissas BlackEyed Pea Salad 247
    Ingredients 247
    Direction 247
    Nutrition Information 247
127. Moms PurpleHull Peas 249
    Ingredients 249
    Direction 249
    Nutrition Information 249
128. My Hoppin John 250
    Ingredients 250
    Direction 250
    Nutrition Information 251
129. Press Box Vegetable Salsa Dip 252
    Ingredients 252
    Direction 252
    Nutrition Information 252
130. Pressure Cooked BlackEyed Peas with Smoked Turkey Leg 254
    Ingredients 254
    Direction 254
    Nutrition Information 255
131. Quick Coconut Curry withRice Corn and Beans 256
    Ingredients 256
    Direction 256
    Nutrition Information 257
132. Quick Corn and Bean Salsa 258

Ingredients 258
Direction 258
Nutrition Information 258
133. Spicy Bean Salsa 260
Ingredients 260
Direction 260
Nutrition Information 260
134. Spicy BlackEyed Pea Soup 262
Ingredients 262
Direction 262
Nutrition Information 263
135. Spinach and Bean Casserole 264
Ingredients 264
Direction 264
Nutrition Information 264
136. Spinach Salad with Hot BaconDressing 266
Ingredients 266
Direction 267
Nutrition Information 267
137. Super Bean Pie 268
Ingredients 268
Direction 269
Nutrition Information 269
138. Sweet and Sour BlackEyedPeas 271
Ingredients 271
Direction 271
Nutrition Information 271
139. Texas Caviar I 273
Ingredients 273
Direction 273
Nutrition Information 273
140. Texas Caviar II 275
Ingredients 275

Direction	275
Nutrition Information	275
141. Three Bean Salad	276
Ingredients	276
Direction	276
142. Toddly Mans Big HouseBlackEyed Peas	278
Ingredients	278
Direction	278
Nutrition Information	279
143. Tutu Dutch Antilles BeanPorridge	280
Ingredients	280
Direction	280
Nutrition Information	280
144. Vegan Cajun Hoppin John	282
Ingredients	282
Direction	282
Nutrition Information	283
145. Vegetarian Southwest OnePotDinner	284
Ingredients	284
Direction	284
Nutrition Information	284
Chapter 3: Fava Beans	286
146. Asturian Beans with Clams	287
Ingredients	287
Direction	287
Nutrition Information	288
147. Besara Egyptian Fava BeanSoup	289
Ingredients	289
Direction	289
Nutrition Information	290
148. Buddha Bowl Power Menu	291
Ingredients	291
Direction	292

Nutrition Information 293
149. Easy Fava Bean Salad 294
Ingredients 294
Direction 294
Nutrition Information 294
150. Easy Mediterranean Pasta 295
Ingredients 295
Direction 295
Nutrition Information 296
151. Fava and Butter Bean Salad 297
Ingredients 297
Direction 297
Nutrition Information 298
152. Fava Bean Dip FoulMudammas 299
Ingredients 299
Direction 299
Nutrition Information 299
153. Fava Bean Hummus withSmoked Trout 301
Ingredients 301
Direction 301
Nutrition Information 302
154. Fava Bean Salad 303
Ingredients 303
Direction 303
Nutrition Information 303
155. Fava Beans 305
Ingredients 305
Direction 305
Nutrition Information 306
156. Fava Beans in Tahini Sauce 307
Ingredients 307
Direction 307
Nutrition Information 307

157. Foul Medammes Spicy FavaBean Dip 309
　　Ingredients 309
　　Direction 309
　　Nutrition Information 310
158. Fresh Fava Beans withHibiscus Salt and Mint 311
　　Ingredients 311
　　Direction 311
　　Nutrition Information 312
159. Green Risotto with FavaBeans 313
　　Ingredients 313
　　Direction 313
　　Nutrition Information 314
160. Grilled Fava Beans 315
　　Ingredients 315
　　Direction 315
　　Nutrition Information 316
161. Jacys MiddleEastern FavaBean Stew 317
　　Ingredients 317
　　Direction 318
　　Nutrition Information 319
162. Jamaican Oxtail with BroadBeans 320
　　Ingredients 320
　　Direction 320
　　Nutrition Information 321
163. Lebanese Bean Salad 322
　　Ingredients 322
　　Direction 322
　　Nutrition Information 322
164. Meze Fava Beans 324
　　Ingredients 324
　　Direction 324
　　Nutrition Information 325
165. Middle Eastern Bean Dip FoulMudammas 326

Ingredients 326
Direction 326
Nutrition Information 327
166. Pasta with Baby Broccoli andBeans 328
Ingredients 328
Direction 328
Nutrition Information 329
167. Persian Sabzi Polo Herb Ricewith Fava Beans 330
Ingredients 330
Direction 330
Nutrition Information 331
168. Portuguese Chourico Beansand Rice 332
Ingredients 332
Direction 332
Nutrition Information 333
169. Portuguese Fava Bean Stew 334
Ingredients 334
Direction 334
Nutrition Information 335
170. Portuguese Favas 336
Ingredients 336
Direction 336
Nutrition Information 336
171. Roasted Kohlrabi Golden Beetand Fava Bean Salad 338
Ingredients 338
Direction 338
Nutrition Information 339
172. Scrumptious Spring Soup 340
Ingredients 340
Direction 341
Nutrition Information 341
173. Swordfish Calabrian Style 342
Ingredients 342

Direction 342
Nutrition Information 343
174. Taameya Egyptian Falafel 344
Ingredients 344
Direction 344
Nutrition Information 345
175. Tuscan Fava Bean and Orecchiette Pasta Salad 346
Ingredients 346
Direction 346
Nutrition Information 347
176. Vegan Fava Bean Salad 348
Ingredients 348
Direction 348
Nutrition Information 348
177. Vegetarian Pumpkin SpinachChili 350
Ingredients 350
Direction 350
Nutrition Information 351

Chapter 1: Black Beans
***

1. Air Fryer Egg Rolls

"Avoid frying by cooking these Southwestern egg rolls in an air fryer and achieving the same crispiness!"

Serving: 16 | Prep: 30 m | Cook: 15 m | Ready in: 45 m

Ingredients

- 2 cups frozen corn, thawed

- 1 (15 ounce) can black beans, drained and rinsed
- 1 (13.5 ounce) can spinach, drained
- 1 1/2 cups shredded jalapeno Jack cheese
- 1 cup sharp Cheddar cheese, shredded
- 1 (4 ounce) can diced green chiles, drained
- 4 green onions, sliced
- 1 teaspoon salt
- 1 teaspoon ground cumin
- 1 teaspoon chili powder
- 1 (16 ounce) package egg roll wrappers

- cooking spray

Direction

- Mix corn, beans, spinach, jalapeno Jack cheese, Cheddar cheese, green chiles, green onions, salt, cumin, and chili powder together in a large bowl for the filling.
- Lay an egg roll wrapper at an angle. Use your finger to lightly moisten all 4 edges with water. Place about 1/4 cup of the filling in the center of the wrapper. Fold 1 corner over filling and tuck in the sides to form a roll. Repeat with remaining wrappers and mist each egg roll with cooking spray.
- Preheat an air fryer to 390 degrees F (199 degrees C). Place egg rolls in the basket, making sure they are not touching; cook in batches if necessary. Fry for 8 minutes; flip and cook until skins are crispy, about 4 minutes more.

Nutrition Information

- Calories: 216 calories
- Total Fat: 7.7 g
- Cholesterol: 25 mg
- Sodium: 628 mg
- Total Carbohydrate: 27 g
- Protein: 10.6 g

2. Alligator Chili

"A Super Bowl favorite that has the bite of a hungry gator."

Serving: 8 | Prep: 20 m | Cook: 2 h 15 m | Ready in: 2 h 35 m

Ingredients

- 1 tablespoon olive oil
- 1 green bell pepper, diced
- 1 sweet onion, diced
- 2 pounds ground alligator meat
- 1 (28 ounce) can crushed tomatoes
- 1 (32 ounce) bottle tomato-vegetable juice cocktail (such as V8®)
- 1 (15 ounce) can black beans, rinsed and drained
- 1 (15 ounce) can kidney beans, rinsed and drained
- 1 tablespoon chipotle chile in adobo sauce, chopped
- 1 tablespoon chili powder
- 1 teaspoon ground cumin
- 1 teaspoon ground cinnamon

- 1 teaspoon smoked paprika
- 1 teaspoon celery salt
- 1/2 teaspoon ground ginger
- salt and pepper to taste
- 1 dash hot sauce, or to taste

Direction

- Heat the olive oil in a large skillet over medium heat. Stir in the green bell pepper and onion; cook and stir until the onion has softened and turned translucent, about 5 minutes. Increase heat to medium-high heat and stir in the ground alligator. Cook and stir until the meat is crumbly, and evenly browned. Drain and discard any excess grease. Stir in the crushed tomatoes, tomato-vegetable juice cocktail, black beans, kidney beans, and chipotle chile. Season with chili powder, cumin, cinnamon, smoked paprika, celery salt, ground ginger, salt, and pepper. Reduce heat to low; cover and simmer for 2 to 3 hours, stirring in water if the chili becomes too thick. Serve with hot sauce.

Nutrition Information

- Calories: 441 calories
- Total Fat: 7.4 g
- Cholesterol: 0 mg
- Sodium: 941 mg
- Total Carbohydrate: 31.9 g
- Protein: 60.8 g

3. Baja Salad

"Favorite ingredients of mine come together as a kitchen sink-style Mexican salad with a crisp, fresh flavor. Goes great with homemade pizza!"

Serving: 6 | Prep: 20 m | Ready in: 20 m

Ingredients

- Salad:
- 1 (12 ounce) package romaine lettuce leaves
- 1 large tomato, diced
- 1 avocado, diced
- 1 pickling cucumber, diced
- 3/4 cup crumbled feta cheese
- 1/4 cup diced red onion
- 1/4 cup white corn kernels
- 1/4 cup cooked black beans
- 1/4 cup crushed tortilla chips, or to taste
- Dressing:
- 2 tablespoons olive oil (optional)

- 2 tablespoons lemon juice (optional)
- 1/4 teaspoon ground cumin (optional)
- salt and ground black pepper to taste (optional)

Direction

- Place romaine lettuce in a large bowl. Add tomato, avocado, cucumber, feta cheese, onion, corn, and black beans; toss well. Sprinkle tortilla chips over salad.
- Whisk olive oil, lemon juice, cumin, salt, and pepper together in a bowl until dressing is smooth; drizzle over salad.

Nutrition Information

- Calories: 223 calories
- Total Fat: 16.8 g
- Cholesterol: 28 mg
- Sodium: 405 mg
- Total Carbohydrate: 13.6 g
- Protein: 7.4 g

4. Baked Chimichangas with Nopales and Poblano

"Low fat because you bake them! Nopales are a type of cactus that you can purchase in the Mexican food section in a jar."

Serving: 8 | Prep: 20 m | Cook: 20 m | Ready in: 40 m

Ingredients

- cooking spray
- 1 poblano chile - halved, seeded, and thinly sliced
- 1/2 medium onion, thinly sliced
- 1 1/2 cups jarred nopales, thinly sliced
- 8 (8 inch) flour tortillas
- 1 cup shredded Monterey Jack cheese
- 1 cup canned black beans, drained and rinsed
- 1 cup plain Greek yogurt, or to taste
- 1 cup salsa, or to taste

Direction

- Preheat the oven to 400 degrees F (200 degrees C). Line a baking sheet with parchment and spray with cooking spray.
- Add poblano chile, onion, and nopales in a skillet over medium-high heat. Cook until chile and onion are soft, 3 to 5 minutes.
- Place 4 tortillas on a microwave-safe plate and cover with a damp paper towel. Heat until soft, about 30 seconds. Repeat with remaining tortillas.
- Place 1 tortilla on a work surface. Spoon 2 tablespoons each of nopales mixture, Monterey Jack cheese, and black beans on

top and fold in sides. Place chimichanga on the prepared baking sheet seam-side down. Repeat with remaining fillings and tortillas.
- Bake in the preheated oven until golden brown, turning halfway through, 15 to 20 minutes.

Nutrition Information

- Calories: 289 calories
- Total Fat: 10.5 g
- Cholesterol: 18 mg
- Sodium: 641 mg
- Total Carbohydrate: 37.1 g
- Protein: 12 g

5. Balela Chickpea and Black Bean Salad

"A quick, simple, and nutritious salad! Balela is a Middle Eastern salad with chickpeas, black

beans, parsley, and spices. There are variations that use mint, cumin, and other flavorings, but

this one is pretty basic. Feel free to experiment! The salad is very healthy with plenty of protein

and fiber from the beans. Serve with good rough peasant bread and red wine."

Serving: 4 | Prep: 15 m | Ready in: 30 m

Ingredients

- 1 (15 ounce) can garbanzo beans (chickpeas), drained
- 1 (15 ounce) can black beans, drained
- 2 ripe tomatoes, chopped
- 1/2 onion, chopped
- 1/2 cup chopped fresh flat-leaf parsley
- 3 tablespoons extra-virgin olive oil
- 1 lemon, juiced
- 1 clove garlic, minced
- 1 pinch salt and fresh coarsely ground black pepper to taste (optional)

Direction

- Combine garbanzo beans, black beans, tomatoes, onion, parsley, olive oil, lemon juice, garlic, salt, and pepper together in a bowl. Allow to sit for flavors to blend, 15 to 30 minutes.

Nutrition Information

- Calories: 300 calories
- Total Fat: 11.5 g
- Cholesterol: 0 mg
- Sodium: 626 mg
- Total Carbohydrate: 39.7 g
- Protein: 11.1 g

6. Beef Enchiladas with Homemade Sauce

"Beef enchiladas with homemade sauce. Top with black olives, mashed avocado, and fresh cilantro!"

Serving: 4 | Prep: 15 m | Cook: 52 m | Ready in: 1 h 7 m

Ingredients

- Enchilada Sauce:
- 3 tablespoons vegetable oil
- 1 tablespoon all-purpose flour
- 2 tablespoons chili powder, or more to taste
- 2 cups chicken stock
- 1 (6 ounce) can tomato paste
- 1 teaspoon dried oregano
- 1 teaspoon ground cumin
- 1/4 teaspoon salt
- Enchiladas:
- cooking spray
- 1 pound ground beef
- 1 teaspoon extra-virgin olive oil
- 1 onion, diced
- 2 (4 ounce) cans fire-roasted diced green chiles
- 1/2 green bell pepper, diced
- 1 (15 ounce) can black beans, rinsed and drained
- 8 low-carb high-fiber tortillas (such as La Tortilla Factory®)
- 1 (8 ounce) package shredded low-fat Mexican cheese blend

Direction

- Heat vegetable oil in a saucepan over medium heat. Add flour; cook and stir using a wooden spoon until smooth, 1 to 2 minutes. Mix in chili powder and cook until fragrant, about 30 seconds. Stir in chicken stock, tomato paste, oregano, cumin, and salt; bring to a boil. Reduce heat and simmer enchilada sauce until thickened and smooth, about 15 minutes.
- Preheat oven to 375 degrees F (190 degrees C). Coat the inside of a 9x13-inch baking dish with cooking spray.
- Heat a large skillet over medium-high heat. Cook and stir beef in the hot skillet until browned and crumbly, 5 to 7 minutes; drain and discard grease.
- Heat olive oil in a separate skillet over medium heat; cook and stir onion, green chiles, and green bell pepper until softened, 5 to 10 minutes. Mix in ground beef and black beans. Stir in 1/2 of the enchilada sauce; cook and stir 1 to 2 minutes.
- Spoon beef mixture evenly onto the center of each tortilla and roll tortilla around filling. Place tortillas, seam-side down, in the baking dish. Cover tortillas with remaining enchilada sauce and Mexican cheese blend.
- Bake in the preheated oven until cheese is melted, about 20 minutes.

Nutrition Information

- Calories: 815 calories
- Total Fat: 44.5 g
- Cholesterol: 113 mg
- Sodium: 2560 mg
- Total Carbohydrate: 62.2 g
- Protein: 48.7 g

7. Beef Taco Noodle Casserole

"Egg noodle casserole recipe with seasoned ground beef, Southwest vegetables, tomatoes and cheese."

Serving: 6 | Prep: 15 m | Ready in: 45 m

Ingredients

- PAM® Original No-Stick Cooking Spray
- 6 ounces dry extra-wide egg noodles, uncooked
- 1 pound ground chuck beef (80% lean)
- 2 cups frozen Southwest mixed vegetables (corn, black beans, red peppers)
- 1 (10 ounce) can Ro*Tel® Original Diced Tomatoes Green Chilies, undrained
- 1 (10 ounce) can red enchilada sauce
- 1 1/4 cups water
- 1 1/4 cups shredded Mexican blend cheese
- 1/4 cup thinly sliced green onions
- Sour cream (optional)

Direction

- Preheat oven to 400 degrees F. Spray 13x9-inch glass baking dish with cooking spray. Place uncooked noodles in baking dish.
- Heat large skillet over medium-high heat. Add beef; cook 5 to 7 minutes or until crumbled and no longer pink. Drain. Add vegetables, undrained tomatoes, enchilada sauce and water to skillet; stir. Bring to a boil. Pour mixture over noodles.

- Cover dish tightly with foil; bake 15 minutes. Stir; sprinkle with cheese and cover with foil. Bake 10 minutes more or until noodles are tender. Sprinkle with green onions. Serve with sour cream, if desired.

Nutrition Information

- Calories: 490 calories
- Total Fat: 25.1 g
- Cholesterol: 101 mg
- Sodium: 520 mg
- Total Carbohydrate: 38 g
- Protein: 26.8 g

8. Best Bean Salad

"I'd turned my nose up at this for years, but suddenly I can't get enough of it. Thanks, Momma D!"

Serving: 18 | Prep: 20 m | Ready in: 8 h 20 m

Ingredients

- 1 (14.5 ounce) can green beans, drained
- 1 (14.5 ounce) can wax beans, drained
- 1 (15.5 ounce) can garbanzo beans, drained
- 1 (14.5 ounce) can kidney beans, drained
- 1 (14.5 ounce) can black beans, drained
- 1/2 cup chopped green pepper
- 1/2 cup chopped onion
- 1/2 cup chopped celery
- 1/2 cup salad oil
- 1/2 cup vinegar
- 1/2 teaspoon salt
- 1/2 teaspoon ground black pepper
- 3/4 cup white sugar

Direction

- Combine the green beans, wax beans, garbanzo beans, kidney beans, green pepper, onion, and celery in a large bowl; toss to mix.
- Whisk together the oil, vinegar, salt, pepper, and sugar in a separate bowl until the sugar is dissolved; pour over the bean mixture. Refrigerate 8 hours or overnight before serving.

Nutrition Information

- Calories: 167 calories
- Total Fat: 6.5 g
- Cholesterol: 0 mg
- Sodium: 412 mg
- Total Carbohydrate: 23.6 g
- Protein: 4.4 g

9. Best Beef Enchiladas

"These enchiladas are absolutely amazing! Truly a recipe your family will love."

Serving: 8 | Prep: 25 m | Cook: 20 m | Ready in: 45 m

Ingredients

- 2 pounds ground beef
- 1/4 onion, finely chopped
- 1 cup shredded Cheddar cheese
- 1/2 cup sour cream
- 1 tablespoon dried parsley
- 1 tablespoon taco seasoning
- 1 teaspoon dried oregano
- 1/2 teaspoon ground black pepper
- 2 1/2 cups enchilada sauce
- 1 1/2 teaspoons chili powder
- 1 clove garlic, minced
- 1/2 teaspoon salt
- 8 flour tortillas
- 1 (15 ounce) can black beans, rinsed and drained
- 1 (4 ounce) can sliced black olives, drained
- 1/4 cup shredded Cheddar cheese

Direction

- Preheat oven to 350 degrees F (175 degrees C).
- Cook and stir ground beef with onion in a skillet over medium heat until meat is crumbly and no longer pink, about 10 minutes. Drain grease. Stir 1 cup Cheddar cheese, sour cream, parsley, taco seasoning, oregano, and black pepper into the

ground beef until cheese has melted. Mix in enchilada sauce, chili powder, garlic, and salt; bring to a simmer, reduce heat to low, and simmer until meat sauce is slightly thickened, about 5 minutes.
- Lay a tortilla onto a work surface and spoon about 1/4 cup of meat sauce down the center of the tortilla. Top meat sauce with 1 tablespoon black beans and a sprinkling of black olives. Roll the tortilla up, enclosing the filling, and lay seam-side down into a 9x13-inch baking dish. Repeat with remaining tortillas. Spoon any remaining meat sauce over the enchiladas and scatter any remaining black beans and black olives over the top. Sprinkle tortillas with 1/4 cup Cheddar cheese.
- Bake in the preheated oven until cheese topping is melted and enchiladas and sauce are bubbling, 20 to 22 minutes. Let stand 5 minutes before serving.

Nutrition Information

- Calories: 583 calories
- Total Fat: 29.2 g
- Cholesterol: 94 mg
- Sodium: 1216 mg
- Total Carbohydrate: 46.1 g
- Protein: 33 g

10. Best Black Beans

"This simple black bean side dish works well with Mexican or Cuban meals."

Serving: 4 | Prep: 10 m | Cook: 5 m | Ready in: 15 m

Ingredients

- 1 (16 ounce) can black beans
- 1 small onion, chopped
- 1 clove garlic, chopped
- 1 tablespoon chopped fresh cilantro
- 1/4 teaspoon cayenne pepper
- salt to taste

Direction

- In a medium saucepan, combine beans, onion, and garlic, and bring to a boil. Reduce heat to medium-low. Season with cilantro, cayenne, and salt. Simmer for 5 minutes, and serve.

Nutrition Information

- Calories: 112 calories
- Total Fat: 0.4 g
- Cholesterol: 0 mg
- Sodium: 510 mg
- Total Carbohydrate: 20.8 g
- Protein: 7.1 g

11. Black Bean and Corn Quesadillas

"My vegetarian husband goes crazy over these every time! They are really cheesy, a little bit spicy, and a little bit sweet. Feel free to play around and add chicken or veggies, if you desire. Don't forget the salsa and sour cream!"

Serving: 8 | Prep: 10 m | Cook: 30 m | Ready in: 40 m

Ingredients

- 2 teaspoons olive oil
- 3 tablespoons finely chopped onion
- 1 (15.5 ounce) can black beans, drained and rinsed
- 1 (10 ounce) can whole kernel corn, drained
- 1 tablespoon brown sugar
- 1/4 cup salsa
- 1/4 teaspoon red pepper flakes
- 2 tablespoons butter, divided
- 8 (8 inch) flour tortillas
- 1 1/2 cups shredded Monterey Jack cheese, divided

Direction

- Heat oil in a large saucepan over medium heat. Stir in onion, and cook until softened, about 2 minutes. Stir in beans and corn, then add sugar, salsa, and pepper flakes; mix well. Cook until heated through, about 3 minutes.
- Melt 2 teaspoons of the butter in a large skillet over medium heat. Place a tortilla in the skillet, sprinkle evenly with cheese, then top with some of the bean mixture. Place another tortilla on top, cook until golden, then flip and cook on the other side.

Melt more butter as needed, and repeat with remaining tortillas and filling.

Nutrition Information

- Calories: 363 calories
- Total Fat: 14.5 g
- Cholesterol: 26 mg
- Sodium: 732 mg
- Total Carbohydrate: 45.6 g
- Protein: 13.9 g

12. Black Bean and Corn Salsa from RED GOLD

"Fresh summer flavors any time of the year! Our tomatoes combined with corn and black beans, green onions and cilantro make the best dip. All you need is a sturdy chip!"

Serving: 30 | Prep: 15 m | Ready in: 15 m

Ingredients

- 2 (15 ounce) cans black beans, drained and rinsed
- 1 (14.5 ounce) can whole kernel corn, drained
- 2 (10 ounce) cans RED GOLD® Petite Diced Tomatoes Green Chilies
- 1 (14.5 ounce) can RED GOLD® Diced Tomatoes, drained
- 1/2 cup chopped green onions
- 2 tablespoons chopped fresh cilantro
- Salt and black pepper to taste

Direction

- In a large bowl combine all ingredients, stir to combine. Refrigerate for several hours or overnight to blend the flavors. Serve with chips or crackers.

Nutrition Information

- Calories: 43 calories
- Total Fat: 0.2 g
- Cholesterol: 0 mg

- Sodium: 226 mg
- Total Carbohydrate: 8.5 g
- Protein: 2.4 g

13. Black Bean and Corn Vegetarian Burger

"My picky vegetarian daughter absolutely loved these black bean and corn vegetarian burgers. Simple and delicious! Serve with your favorite burger condiments and vegetables."

Serving: 15 | Prep: 45 m | Cook: 14 m | Ready in: 59 m

Ingredients

- 1 pound toasted almonds, chopped
- 6 cups instant oatmeal
- 2 cups ketchup
- 1 (12 ounce) package frozen corn kernels, thawed
- 4 eggs, beaten
- 1 cup chopped mushrooms
- 1/2 cup red bell pepper, finely diced
- 1/2 cup minced red onion
- 6 green onions, thinly sliced
- 6 tablespoons olive oil
- 2 tablespoons prepared horseradish
- 1/4 cup Worcestershire sauce
- 1 tablespoon red pepper flakes
- 1 tablespoon dried basil
- 1 tablespoon salt
- 1 teaspoon freshly ground black pepper
- 1 (15 ounce) can black beans, rinsed and drained
- cooking spray

Direction

- Combine almonds, instant oatmeal, ketchup, corn, eggs, mushrooms, red bell pepper, red onion, green onions, olive oil, and horseradish in a bowl. Season with Worcestershire sauce, red pepper flakes, basil, salt, and pepper.
- Fold black beans into the almond mixture, being careful not to smash them. Scoop up 1/2 cup of the mixture; lightly flatten between the palms of your hands to form a patty. Repeat with remaining mixture.
- Coat a skillet lightly with cooking spray and heat over medium heat. Place patties in the hot skillet and cook until browned, about 7 minutes per side.

Nutrition Information

- Calories: 456 calories
- Total Fat: 25.1 g
- Cholesterol: 44 mg
- Sodium: 1083 mg
- Total Carbohydrate: 48 g
- Protein: 15.7 g

14. Black Bean and Potato Veggie Burgers

"The hubby and I are trying to eat less meat, more veggies. These hold together very well, have good flavor and are very moist. After the first bite the hubby asked me to write down the recipe before anything was forgotten. I look forward to seeing the tweaks people will make to improve on a good base. Enjoy!"

Serving: 8 | Prep: 25 m | Cook: 10 m | Ready in: 35 m

Ingredients

- 4 baked potatoes
- 1 (15 ounce) can black beans, rinsed and drained
- 1/2 onion, finely chopped
- 1/2 carrot, grated
- 1/2 green bell pepper, finely chopped
- 6 mushrooms, finely chopped
- 2 cloves garlic, minced
- 1 tablespoon Worcestershire sauce
- 1 tablespoon ground cumin
- 1 tablespoon chili powder
- 1 teaspoon hot sauce
- salt and ground black pepper to taste
- 3 tablespoons olive oil, divided

Direction

- Mash potatoes and black beans together in a large bowl, removing any large pieces of potato skin if desired. Mix onion, carrot, green pepper, mushrooms, and garlic into potato mixture with a fork, mashing until well-mixed.

- Stir Worcestershire sauce, cumin, chili powder, hot sauce, salt, and black pepper into potato mixture. Form mixture into 8 patties.
- Working in batches, heat 1 tablespoon olive oil in a large nonstick skillet over medium-high heat. Cook patties in hot oil until golden and set on the bottom, 4 to 5 minutes; flip each burger and cook until golden and hot throughout, about 4 minutes more.

Nutrition Information

- Calories: 207 calories
- Total Fat: 5.8 g
- Cholesterol: 0 mg
- Sodium: 274 mg
- Total Carbohydrate: 34.2 g
- Protein: 6.7 g

15. Black Bean and White Corn Salad

"A favorite of our family. Excellent to accompany a Mexican-themed meal."

Serving: 4 | Prep: 15 m | Ready in: 15 m

Ingredients

- 1 (16 ounce) package frozen white corn, thawed
- 1 (15 ounce) can black beans, rinsed and drained
- 2 tomatoes, diced
- 1/2 red bell pepper, diced, or more to taste
- 1/3 red onion, diced, or more to taste
- 1/3 cup chopped fresh cilantro, or more to taste
- 1/4 cup fresh lime juice
- 2 teaspoons white tequila
- salt and ground black pepper to taste

Direction

- Mix white corn, black beans, tomatoes, red bell pepper, red onion, cilantro, lime juice, tequila, salt, and black pepper in a large salad bowl.

Nutrition Information

- Calories: 228 calories
- Total Fat: 1.4 g
- Cholesterol: 0 mg
- Sodium: 418 mg

- Total Carbohydrate: 47.3 g
- Protein: 10.9 g

16. Black Bean Breakfast Bowl

"A quick breakfast if you're trying to avoid carbs."

Serving: 2 | Prep: 10 m | Cook: 5 m | Ready in: 15 m

Ingredients

- 2 tablespoons olive oil
- 4 eggs, beaten
- 1 (15 ounce) can black beans, drained and rinsed
- 1 avocado, peeled and sliced
- 1/4 cup salsa
- salt and ground black pepper to taste

Direction

- Heat olive oil in a small pan over medium heat. Cook and stir eggs until eggs are set, 3 to 5 minutes.
- Place black beans in a microwave-safe bowl. Heat on High in the microwave until warm, about 1 minute.
- Divide warmed black beans between two bowls.
- Top each bowl with scrambled eggs, avocado, and salsa. Season with salt and black pepper.

Nutrition Information

- Calories: 625 calories
- Total Fat: 38.8 g
- Cholesterol: 372 mg
- Sodium: 1158 mg

- Total Carbohydrate: 46.6 g
- Protein: 27.9 g

17. Black Bean Cigars

"I created this one night out of whatever I had on hand that I thought might taste good together--my husband thinks I'm a genius now! We named them 'cigars' because they're shaped like cigars, and if you blow into one end, smoke billows out the other!"

Serving: 12 | Prep: 15 m | Cook: 30 m | Ready in: 45 m

Ingredients

- 24 frozen potato rounds, thawed and mashed slightly
- 1 large tomato, diced
- 1/4 cup chopped fresh cilantro
- 1 (15 ounce) can black beans, rinsed and drained
- 1 (8 ounce) container sour cream
- 2 cups shredded Colby-Jack cheese
- 1/2 cup picante sauce
- 1/2 tablespoon chili powder
- 1 pinch cayenne pepper
- 12 (8 inch) flour tortillas

Direction

- Preheat the oven to 425 degrees F (220 degrees C). Coat a 9x13 inch baking dish with cooking spray.
- In a large bowl, mix together the potato rounds, tomato, cilantro, black beans, sour cream, shredded cheese, picante sauce, chili powder and cayenne pepper. Spoon about 1/3 cup of the mixture into each tortilla, and roll up. Place filled tortillas seam side down in the prepared baking dish. Spray the tops of

the tortilla rolls with cooking spray. Cover the dish with aluminum foil.
- Bake for 15 minutes in the preheated oven, remove foil, and continue baking for another 15 minutes, or until golden. Let stand for 5 minutes to set before serving.

Nutrition Information

- Calories: 318 calories
- Total Fat: 16.2 g
- Cholesterol: 30 mg
- Sodium: 541 mg
- Total Carbohydrate: 33.6 g
- Protein: 10.6 g

18. Black Bean Corn and Tomato Salad with Feta Cheese

"I tasted many salads with similar ingredients, but all seemed very bland, so I developed this myself. It is dressed with a lime vinaigrette and has lots of crunch and flavor with a little jalapeno pop. It's wonderful to make in summer with fresh ingredients from the garden or farmer's market. This is great with BBQ's or for potlucks. My husband likes it best with fish tacos."

Serving: 12 | Prep: 1 h | Ready in: 9 h

Ingredients

- 1 (14 ounce) can black beans, drained and rinsed
- 2 fresh tomatoes, chopped
- 1 large green bell pepper, chopped
- 1 cup fresh sweet white corn, cut from the cob
- 1 bunch green onions, sliced
- 1 jicama, peeled and minced
- 1 fresh jalapeno pepper, minced
- 1 (8 ounce) package crumbled feta cheese
- 1 clove garlic
- 1 pinch sea salt
- 1/4 cup fresh lime juice
- 1 teaspoon Dijon mustard
- 1/4 teaspoon fresh-ground black pepper
- 1 cup olive oil

Direction

- Place the beans, tomato, bell pepper, corn, onion, jicama, jalapeno pepper, and feta cheese in a large salad bowl.

- Mash the garlic and salt together with a mortar and pestle. Whisk together the mashed garlic, lime juice, mustard, and pepper in a small bowl. Add the oil in a slow, steady stream while whisking. Continue whisking until smooth. Drizzle the dressing over the salad and toss to coat. Chill overnight.

Nutrition Information

- Calories: 285 calories
- Total Fat: 22.4 g
- Cholesterol: 17 mg
- Sodium: 384 mg
- Total Carbohydrate: 16.8 g
- Protein: 6.1 g

19. Black Bean Quinoa Burgers

"These burgers make up a complete vegetarian protein, and are both delicious and low fat. Add all your burger fixings to your bun, serve, and enjoy."

Serving: 4 | Prep: 20 m | Cook: 33 m | Ready in: 53 m

Ingredients

- 1/2 cup uncooked quinoa
- 1 cup water
- 2 tablespoons vegetable oil, or as needed, divided
- 1 small red onion, chopped
- 1 clove garlic, minced
- 1 cup frozen corn
- 1/3 teaspoon chili powder
- 1/8 teaspoon ground cumin
- 1/8 teaspoon ground cayenne pepper, or to taste (optional)
- salt and ground black pepper to taste
- 1 (15 ounce) can black beans, rinsed and drained
- 2 eggs
- 1/3 cup dry bread crumbs

Direction

- Combine water and quinoa in a pot. Bring to a boil; simmer until water is absorbed, 10 to 15 minutes.
- Heat 1 tablespoon oil in a saucepan over medium heat. Add onion and garlic; cook and stir until onion is translucent and soft, about 5 minutes. Add corn, chili powder, cumin, cayenne pepper, salt, and black pepper. Cook and stir until corn is defrosted, about 5 minutes.

- Mash beans in a bowl using a fork. Add quinoa and corn mixture; mash until well combined. Add eggs; mix well. Stir in bread crumbs. Form mixture into 4 flat, round patties.
- Heat the remaining 1 tablespoon oil in a skillet; cook patties until golden brown, about 4 minutes per side.

Nutrition Information

- Calories: 352 calories
- Total Fat: 11.8 g
- Cholesterol: 93 mg
- Sodium: 555 mg
- Total Carbohydrate: 48.5 g
- Protein: 15.3 g

20. Black Bean Salsa Soup

"This soup tastes just like fresh salsa, one of my favorites! You could add jalapeno or chilies to make it spicy; this version is mild."

Serving: 6 | Prep: 15 m | Cook: 40 m | Ready in: 55 m

Ingredients

- 2 tablespoons butter
- 1/2 cup chopped carrots
- 1/2 cup chopped celery
- 1/2 cup chopped onion
- 1 (48 fluid ounce) can chicken broth
- 1 (14.5 ounce) can diced tomatoes with green chile peppers
- 3 (15 ounce) cans black beans, drained and rinsed
- 1/4 cup cooking sherry
- 1 teaspoon minced garlic
- 1 teaspoon ground cumin
- 1/2 teaspoon ground cayenne pepper
- salt to taste
- 1/2 cup chopped fresh cilantro

Direction

- Melt the butter in a large pot over medium heat. Stir in the carrots, celery, and onion, and cook 15 minutes. Pour in chicken broth. Mix in diced tomatoes with green chile peppers, black beans, sherry, and garlic. Season with cumin, cayenne pepper, and salt. Bring to a boil, reduce heat to low, and simmer 20 minutes. Mix in cilantro during last few minutes of cook time.

Nutrition Information

- Calories: 87 calories
- Total Fat: 4.7 g
- Cholesterol: 16 mg
- Sodium: 1904 mg
- Total Carbohydrate: 8.4 g
- Protein: 2.2 g

21. Black Bean Soup with Rice and Sherry

"Takes a very long time -- but it's worth it."

Serving: 6 | Prep: 8 h | Cook: 8 h | Ready in: 16 h

Ingredients

- 1 cup dry black beans
- 1 quart beef broth
- 1 quart chicken broth
- 1/2 pound smoked ham hock
- 1 large onion, sliced
- 1 carrot, sliced
- 4 sprigs fresh parsley
- 2 cloves garlic
- 1 teaspoon ground thyme
- salt and pepper to taste
- 1 1/2 cups uncooked white rice
- 1/2 cup dry sherry
- 1 small red onion, diced

Direction

- Place beans in a large bowl and cover with several inches of water. Let soak 8 hours or overnight.
- Drain and rinse beans and place in a large pot over medium heat with beef broth, chicken broth, ham hock, onion, carrot, parsley, garlic and thyme. Bring to a boil, then reduce heat, cover and simmer 6 to 8 hours.

- Strain soup into a large saucepan, reserving bean mixture. Remove ham hock and discard. Puree bean mixture in a blender or food processor until smooth. Stir into reserved broth. Cook over low heat 2 hours. Season with salt and pepper.
- In the last 20 minutes of cooking, bring 2 1/2 cups of water to a boil in a medium saucepan. Stir in rice. Reduce heat, cover and cook 20 minutes.
- Ladle soup into six bowls. Top with cooked rice, a spoonful of sherry and a sprinkling of red onion.

Nutrition Information

- Calories: 436 calories
- Total Fat: 9.3 g
- Cholesterol: 26 mg
- Sodium: 682 mg
- Total Carbohydrate: 66 g
- Protein: 19.8 g

22. Black Bean Stuffed Peppers

"What more can you ask for? If my kiddos love this dish, then you know it will be a huge hit in your home. If you have leftover filling, it makes a great chip dip!"

Serving: 6 | Prep: 20 m | Cook: 35 m | Ready in: 55 m

Ingredients

- 1 1/4 cups water
- 1 (3 ounce) package reduced-fat cream cheese, softened
- 2 cups cooked brown rice
- 2 cups chopped fresh spinach
- 1 (10 ounce) can diced tomatoes with green chile peppers
- 1 (15 ounce) can no-salt-added black beans, drained and rinsed
- 2 tablespoons dried minced onion
- 1 teaspoon ground cumin
- 1 teaspoon dried oregano
- 3 large bell peppers
- 1/2 cup shredded Cheddar cheese

Direction

- Preheat oven to 350 degrees F (175 degrees C). Pour water into a 9x13-inch baking dish.
- Stir cream cheese in a bowl until smooth. Fold brown rice, spinach, diced tomatoes with green chiles, black beans, minced onion, cumin, and oregano into the cream cheese until evenly mixed.
- Halve bell peppers lengthwise. Remove and discard stem, seeds, and membranes.

- Fill each pepper half with about 3/4 cup of rice mixture; arrange into baking dish. Sprinkle cheese evenly over stuffed pepper halves.
- Bake in preheated oven until peppers are tender, 35 to 45 minutes.

Nutrition Information

- Calories: 230 calories
- Total Fat: 6.5 g
- Cholesterol: 18 mg
- Sodium: 309 mg
- Total Carbohydrate: 33.4 g
- Protein: 10.7 g

23. Black Beans and Pork Chops

"A hearty dinner, great with rice! It is one of family's favorite dinners given to me by my sister. You may adjust amounts of beans and salsa to your preference. I always seem to add more!"

Serving: 4 | Prep: 5 m | Cook: 25 m | Ready in: 30 m

Ingredients

- 4 bone-in pork chops
- ground black pepper to taste
- 1 tablespoon olive oil
- 1 (15 ounce) can black beans, with liquid
- 1 cup salsa
- 1 tablespoon chopped fresh cilantro

Direction

- Season pork chops with pepper.
- Heat oil in a large skillet over medium-high heat. Cook pork chops in hot oil until browned, 3 to 5 minutes per side.
- Pour beans and salsa over pork chops and season with cilantro. Bring to a boil, reduce heat to medium-low, cover the skillet, and simmer until pork chops are cooked no longer pink in the center, 20 to 35 minutes. An instant-read thermometer inserted into the center should read 145 degrees F (63 degrees C).

Nutrition Information

- Calories: 392 calories

- Total Fat: 18.7 g
- Cholesterol: 72 mg
- Sodium: 837 mg
- Total Carbohydrate: 21.8 g
- Protein: 33.8 g

24. Bulgur Chili

"Healthy meat-free chili."

Serving: 10 | Prep: 30 m | Cook: 48 m | Ready in: 1 h 18 m

Ingredients

- 2 cups water
- 1 cup bulgur
- 1 tablespoon olive oil
- 2 cups shredded carrots
- 1 large onion, chopped
- 1 green bell pepper, chopped
- 1 red bell pepper, chopped
- 1/2 jalapeno pepper, seeded and minced
- 2 cloves garlic, minced, or more to taste
- 5 cups reduced-sodium tomato juice
- 2 (16 ounce) cans kidney beans
- 2 (16 ounce) cans black beans
- 1 (28 ounce) can petite diced tomatoes, undrained
- 1 (8 ounce) can low-sodium tomato sauce
- 2 tablespoons chili powder
- 2 tablespoons taco seasoning
- 1 1/2 teaspoons ground cumin
- 1/4 teaspoon cayenne pepper
- 1/4 teaspoon ground black pepper

Direction

- Pour water and bulgur into a saucepan. Bring to a boil; cover and simmer until tender, 12 to 15 minutes. Drain off excess

water.
- Heat olive oil in a large pot over medium heat. Add carrots, onions, green bell pepper, red bell pepper, and jalapeno pepper; cook and stir until softened and starting to brown, 5 to 10 minutes. Stir in garlic; cook and stir until fragrant, 1 to 2 minutes.
- Stir cooked bulgur, tomato juice, kidney beans, black beans, diced tomatoes, tomato sauce, chili powder, taco seasoning, cumin, cayenne, and pepper into the pot. Bring to a boil; reduce heat and simmer until flavors combine, 20 to 30 minutes.

Nutrition Information

- Calories: 297 calories
- Total Fat: 2.7 g
- Cholesterol: 0 mg
- Sodium: 848 mg
- Total Carbohydrate: 56.1 g
- Protein: 14.8 g

25. Candices Butternut Squash Enchiladas

"Butternut squash enchiladas, vegetarian-friendly."

Serving: 6 | Prep: 20 m | Cook: 40 m | Ready in: 1 h

Ingredients

- 1 butternut squash - peeled, halved lengthwise, and seeded
- 1/4 cup vegetable oil for frying, or as needed
- 12 corn tortillas
- 1 (28 ounce) can enchilada sauce
- 1/2 teaspoon ground cinnamon
- 1/2 teaspoon garlic salt (optional)
- 1/2 teaspoon ground black pepper
- 1/2 (15 ounce) can black beans, rinsed and drained
- 1/3 cup chopped fresh cilantro
- 1 cup shredded Colby-Jack cheese

Direction

- Place squash halves in a microwave-safe bowl and cover bowl with plastic wrap. Cook in microwave until flesh is very tender, 12 to 15 minutes.
- Pour about 1 inch of oil in a skillet and place over medium-low heat. Fry tortillas in oil until softened and lightly browned, about 10 seconds per side. Drain tortillas on paper towel-lined plates.
- Preheat oven to 325 degrees F (165 degrees C).
- Spread a thin layer of enchilada sauce into the bottom of a 9x13-inch baking dish.

- Sprinkle cinnamon, garlic salt, and black pepper over squash; mash until smooth. Stir black beans and cilantro into squash mixture until filling is well mixed.
- Place a tortilla in the bottom of the baking dish; spoon filling down the middle and roll tortilla around filling, keeping it seam-side down. Repeat with remaining tortillas and filling. Stack rolled tortillas on top of each other, if needed. Pour remaining enchilada sauce over tortillas and top with Colby-Jack cheese.
- Bake in the preheated oven until cheese is melted, 25 to 30 minutes.

Nutrition Information

- Calories: 384 calories
- Total Fat: 12.5 g
- Cholesterol: 22 mg
- Sodium: 830 mg
- Total Carbohydrate: 58.9 g
- Protein: 13.9 g

26. Caribbean Wrap

"Quick, easy, and packs well for picnics."

Serving: 4 | Prep: 35 m | Ready in: 35 m

Ingredients

- 2 cups shredded breast meat from a rotisserie chicken
- 2 cups cubed mango
- 1 cup low-sodium black beans, rinsed and drained
- 1/2 cup chopped red onion
- 2 2/3 tablespoons chopped fresh cilantro
- 8 cloves garlic, chopped
- 1 pinch red pepper flakes
- 4 (8 inch) low-fat whole wheat tortillas
- 8 cups mixed salad greens
- 3 tablespoons Italian salad dressing, or to taste
- 1/2 cup roasted macadamia nuts

Direction

- Combine chicken, mango, black beans, red onion, cilantro, garlic, and red pepper flakes in a large bowl.
- Divide chicken mixture among tortillas. Roll up tortillas.
- Toss salad greens with dressing in a large bowl; garnish with macadamia nuts. Serve each wrap with 2 cups of salad.

Nutrition Information

- Calories: 490 calories

- Total Fat: 25.5 g
- Cholesterol: 55 mg
- Sodium: 492 mg
- Total Carbohydrate: 47.3 g
- Protein: 28 g

27. Chicken and Black Bean Chili

"This a recipe I came up with after getting a few ideas from a friend. The combination of chipotle and cilantro really complete this chili."

Serving: 6 | Prep: 15 m | Cook: 1 h | Ready in: 1 h 15 m

Ingredients

- 2 tablespoons cooking oil
- 3 large skinless, boneless chicken breast halves - cut into 1 inch pieces
- sea salt to taste
- 1 tablespoon chili powder, or to taste
- 1/2 tablespoon ground cumin, or to taste
- 1 dried chipotle chili pepper, ground into powder
- ground black pepper to taste
- 1/2 teaspoon ground cayenne pepper
- 1 small yellow onion, diced
- 1 medium green bell pepper, diced
- 1 medium yellow bell pepper, diced
- 5 cups water
- 1 (15 ounce) can kidney beans, undrained
- 1 (15 ounce) can black beans, undrained
- 1 (11 ounce) can whole kernel corn, drained
- 1 teaspoon green pepper sauce (e.g., Tabasco®)
- 1 (6 ounce) can roasted garlic tomato paste
- 1 bunch fresh cilantro, chopped

Direction

- Heat the oil in a large pot over medium heat. Place chicken in the pot; brown on all sides. Season with sea salt, chili powder, cumin, ground chipotle, black pepper, and cayenne pepper. Mix in onion, green bell pepper, and yellow bell pepper. Pour in about 3 cups water, and continue cooking 10 minutes, until about 1/2 the water has evaporated.
- Mix the kidney beans, black beans, and corn into the pot. Season with green pepper sauce. Reduce heat to low, and mix in remaining 2 cups water and tomato paste. Simmer, stirring occasionally 30 minutes, or until thickened. Top with cilantro to serve.

Nutrition Information

- Calories: 310 calories
- Total Fat: 8.5 g
- Cholesterol: 59 mg
- Sodium: 712 mg
- Total Carbohydrate: 30.5 g
- Protein: 29.1 g

28. Chicken and Two Bean Chili

"An awesome change from the traditional beef chili! I made this for my husband for the first time and he went back for seconds!"

Serving: 8 | Prep: 20 m | Cook: 3 h 35 m | Ready in: 3 h 55 m

Ingredients

- 2 chicken breasts, cut into chunks
- 1 tablespoon olive oil
- 1/3 red onion, chopped
- 3 cloves garlic, minced
- 1 (15 ounce) can black beans, drained
- 1 (14.5 ounce) can great Northern beans, drained
- 2 (14.5 ounce) cans diced tomatoes with green chile peppers
- 1 (14 ounce) can tomato sauce
- 1/2 cup chicken stock
- 1/2 cup brown sugar
- 1/2 cup frozen corn
- 1/4 cup white vinegar
- 3 tablespoons chili powder
- 3 tablespoons ground cumin
- 2 tablespoons dried cilantro
- Dash of salt
- 1 pinch cayenne pepper
- 1/2 green bell peppers, diced
- 1/2 red bell pepper, diced
- 1/2 yellow bell pepper, diced

Direction

- Fill a large pot with lightly-salted water and bring to a boil. Boil the chicken until no longer pink in the center and the juices run clear, 7 to 10 minutes. Drain the chicken and place in a slow cooker.
- Heat the olive oil in a skillet over medium heat. Brown the onion and garlic in the hot oil, 5 to 7 minutes; scrape into the slow cooker.
- Add the black beans, great Northern beans, tomatoes with green chiles, tomato sauce, chicken stock, brown sugar, corn, vinegar, chili powder, cumin, cilantro, salt, and cayenne pepper to the slow cooker. Cook on High until the beans are tender, 3 to 4 hours. Stir the diced green, red, and yellow bell peppers into the chili and cook another 20 minutes.

Nutrition Information

- Calories: 219 calories
- Total Fat: 3.8 g
- Cholesterol: 15 mg
- Sodium: 813 mg
- Total Carbohydrate: 37.6 g
- Protein: 12.2 g

29. Chicken Nachos from Reynolds Wrap

"Make this fun and kid-friendly appetizer in 30 minutes or less!"

Serving: 6 | Prep: 20 m | Cook: 4 h | Ready in: 4 h 20 m

Ingredients

- 4 boneless, skinless chicken breasts
- 1 (14 ounce) can enchilada sauce
- 1 (12 ounce) package tortilla chips
- 1 (14 ounce) can black beans, rinsed and drained
- Shredded Mexican blend cheese
- Sliced black olives
- Salsa
- Avocados
- Banana peppers
- 1 Reynolds® Slow Cooker Liner
- Reynolds Wrap® Non Stick Aluminum Foil

Direction

- Line a 5 to 6-quart slow cooker with a Reynolds(R) Slow Cooker Liner. Open slow cooker liner and place it inside a slow cooker bowl. Fit liner snugly against the bottom and sides of bowl; pull top of liner over rim of bowl.
- Place chicken in slow cooker. Top with 1 can of enchilada sauce.
- Cover the slow cooker and cook on low for 4-6 hours.

- Carefully remove lid to allow steam to escape. Remove the chicken and place on a cutting board. Use two forks to shred, or use your stand mixer to help speed up the process. Place the chicken in the mixer and turn the mixer to low for about 30 seconds. Cool slow cooker completely; remove liner and toss.
- Preheat oven to 350 degrees F (175 degrees C). Line a cookie sheet with the Reynolds Wrap(R) Non-Stick Foil, facing the dull side up.
- Line the foil with tortilla chips and top with the chicken, black beans and shredded cheese. Bake for about 10 minutes, until the cheese is all melted. Remove nachos from oven and top with sliced olives, salsa, avocados, banana peppers and any other fixings of your choosing!

Nutrition Information

- Calories: 631 calories
- Total Fat: 31.4 g
- Cholesterol: 62 mg
- Sodium: 1339 mg
- Total Carbohydrate: 60.2 g
- Protein: 31.2 g

30. Chicken Tortilla Soup IV

"Loaded with corn and beans, this soup is hearty enough for a main meal. Save time by topping it with purchased tortilla chips."

Serving: 6

Ingredients

- 2 1/2 teaspoons vegetable oil
- 6 (6 inch) corn tortillas, cut into 1/2 inch strips
- 3 cups chicken broth
- 1/2 teaspoon ground cumin
- 1/2 teaspoon chili powder
- 1/2 teaspoon dried oregano
- 1 (15 ounce) can black beans, rinsed and drained
- 1 (15 ounce) can whole kernel corn, drained
- 2 skinless, boneless chicken breast halves, cut into bite size pieces
- 1/2 cup salsa
- 1/2 cup chopped fresh cilantro

Direction

- Heat 2 teaspoons of the oil in a large pot over medium heat. Add half of the tortilla strips, stirring often, until crisp. Drain on paper towels. Repeat with remaining 1/2 teaspoon of oil and remaining tortilla strips and set aside.
- Add the broth, cumin, chili powder and oregano to the pot. Raise heat to high and bring to a boil. Add the beans, corn, chicken and salsa. Reduce heat to low, stir and simmer for

about 2 minutes, or until chicken is cooked through and no longer pink inside.
- Add the cilantro and half of the reserved tortilla strips. Ladle into individual bowls and garnish each bowl with some of the remaining strips.

Nutrition Information

- Calories: 257 calories
- Total Fat: 5.5 g
- Cholesterol: 20 mg
- Sodium: 968 mg
- Total Carbohydrate: 36.1 g
- Protein: 17.6 g

31. Coconut Rice with Black Beans

"Easy, delicious rice and bean dish that can be served as a main vegetarian course or side dish to Latin and Asian foods."

Serving: 6 | Prep: 5 m | Cook: 25 m | Ready in: 30 m

Ingredients

- 1 tablespoon butter
- 1/2 shallot, minced
- 1 cup uncooked jasmine rice
- 3/4 cup coconut milk
- 1 cup water
- 1 pinch ground nutmeg
- 1 (15 ounce) can black beans, rinsed and drained

Direction

- Melt the butter in a small saucepan over medium heat. Stir in the shallot, and cook until the shallot has softened and turned translucent, about 3 minutes. Add the rice and stir until coated with the butter. Pour in the coconut milk and water; season with nutmeg. Bring to a boil over high heat, then reduce heat to medium-low, cover, and simmer until the liquid has been absorbed and the rice is tender, about 18 minutes. Stir in the black beans, and cook a few minutes until hot.

Nutrition Information

- Calories: 190 calories
- Total Fat: 8 g
- Cholesterol: 5 mg
- Sodium: 19 mg
- Total Carbohydrate: 27.2 g
- Protein: 2.8 g

32. Corned Beef Hash Breakfast Tacos

"An easy breakfast taco recipe using corned beef hash instead of bacon or sausage."

Serving: 4 | Prep: 5 m | Cook: 12 m | Ready in: 17 m

Ingredients

- 1 (15 ounce) can HORMEL® Mary Kitchen® Corned Beef Hash
- 1 (15 ounce) can black beans, rinsed and drained
- 1/4 teaspoon garlic powder
- 1/4 teaspoon chili powder
- Salt to taste (optional)
- 1/8 teaspoon ground black pepper
- 1 teaspoon vegetable oil
- 4 eggs, beaten
- 10 (6 inch) soft flour tortillas
- 1/4 cup pico de gallo salsa, or to taste
- 1/4 cup shredded Mexican cheese blend, or more to taste
- 1/4 cup sour cream, or to taste
- 1/4 cup chopped fresh cilantro, or to taste
- 1 lime, cut into wedges (optional)

Direction

- Mix corned beef hash, black beans, garlic powder, chili powder, salt, and pepper in a saucepan. Cook on medium-high heat for

about 8-10 minutes, stirring occasionally, until bubbly and meat starts to brown. Transfer to a warm dish.
- Heat oil in skillet over medium to medium-high heat. Pour in eggs. Cook and stir, lifting up edges of eggs to let uncooked egg reach skillet surface. Remove from heat when eggs are still slightly glossy or to desired doneness, about 4 minutes.
- Distribute the corned beef hash mixture onto the flour tortillas. Top with scrambled eggs, salsa, cheese, sour cream, and cilantro.
- Garnish with lime wedges, if desired.

Nutrition Information

- Calories: 655 calories
- Total Fat: 27.7 g
- Cholesterol: 203 mg
- Sodium: 1586 mg
- Total Carbohydrate: 72.5 g
- Protein: 28.9 g

33. Cottage Cheese Avocado and Black Bean Salsa

"This may look and sound sort of bad, but let me tell you, there isn't a tastier, nutritious, salsa-like dip to hold you over while you wait for dinner. Funny enough, this was created as an experiment with leftovers, and now I have over 15 friends making it on a regular basis! This is a great recipe that can be stored in the refrigerator for several days for a quick, anytime snack. (Frozen corn, heated and cooled in the same manner, may be used in place of the corn on the cob.)"

Serving: 10 | Prep: 15 m | Cook: 15 m | Ready in: 30 m

Ingredients

- 1 ear corn, husked and cleaned
- 1 (15 ounce) can reduced sodium black beans
- 1 (32 ounce) container 1% fat cottage cheese
- 1 avocado - peeled, pitted, and diced
- 2 roma (plum) tomatoes, seeded and diced
- 2 cups salsa
- 1 (13.5 ounce) package tortilla chips, if desired

Direction

- Place corn on the cob in a microwave safe dish with 1/4 inch of water. Cover, and microwave on medium high for 4 minutes, or until tender. Cool under running water, and slice kernels from cob. Set aside.
- Cook the black beans in a small saucepan over medium heat until warm and tender, about 10 minutes. Strain, and rinse under cold water to remove liquid and excess sodium. Set aside.

- Place the cottage cheese in a mixing or serving bowl. Peel, pit, and dice the avocado into bite size pieces, and add to the cottage cheese. Cut the tomatoes in half lengthwise, remove seeds, and dice into bite size pieces. Add to the cottage cheese along with the corn, black beans, and salsa. Stir until well blended. Cover and refrigerate until ready to serve. Serve with tortilla chips, if desired.

Nutrition Information

- Calories: 334 calories
- Total Fat: 12.9 g
- Cholesterol: 3 mg
- Sodium: 907 mg
- Total Carbohydrate: 41.8 g
- Protein: 17 g

34. Double Crust Bean Pie

"Black beans, cheese, bell peppers, onion and spices baked between 2 pie crusts."

Serving: 6 | Prep: 10 m | Cook: 1 h 15 m | Ready in: 1 h 25 m

Ingredients

- 1 tablespoon vegetable oil
- 1 onion, finely chopped
- 1 small green bell pepper, chopped
- 1 (15 ounce) can black beans, drained
- 1/3 cup salsa
- 1/4 cup chopped red bell pepper
- 3/4 teaspoon chili powder
- 1/4 teaspoon cayenne pepper
- 1/4 teaspoon ground black pepper
- 2 (9 inch) unbaked 9 inch pie crusts
- 1 1/2 cups shredded Cheddar cheese

Direction

- Preheat oven to 325 degrees F (165 degrees C).
- Heat oil in a medium saucepan over medium heat. Sauté onion and green pepper until tender. Sir in beans, salsa, red bell pepper, chili powder, cayenne and black pepper. Reduce heat to low and simmer for 15 minutes.
- Spoon half of the mixture into one of the pie crusts and cover with half of the cheese. Repeat with remaining beans and cheese. Top with remaining crust.
- Bake in preheated oven for 1 hour.

Nutrition Information

- Calories: 456 calories
- Total Fat: 31.7 g
- Cholesterol: 30 mg
- Sodium: 578 mg
- Total Carbohydrate: 32 g
- Protein: 11.4 g

35. Easy Black Beans and Rice

"Black Beans and Rice is the perfect family side dish. It's fast and affordable, and everyone loves the taste. A black bean and rice dish is more than satisfying, too-- it's packed with protein for a healthy meal. Our recipe for rice and beans can't be easier. You make it with GOYA® Canned Beans, so you won't mind when your family requests it again and again."

Serving: 4 | Prep: 5 m | Cook: 10 m | Ready in: 15 m

Ingredients

- 1 (15.5 ounce) can Goya Black Beans, undrained
- 1 tablespoon Goya Extra Virgin Olive Oil
- 1 tablespoon Goya Golden Cooking Wine
- 1 tablespoon Goya Recaito
- 1 Goya Bay Leaf
- 1 packet Sazon Goya without Annatto
- 1/2 teaspoon brown sugar
- 1/2 teaspoon Goya Oregano Leaf, or to taste
- 1/2 teaspoon Goya White Vinegar
- 1/4 teaspoon Goya Cumin, or to taste
- Goya Adobo with Pepper, to taste
- 2 cups cooked Canilla Extra Long Grain Rice

Direction

- Add 1/4 cup water to 4 quart saucepan over medium heat. Add first 10 ingredients to pot. Bring bean mixture to a boil. Reduce heat to medium-low and simmer until flavors come together, about 10 minutes. Discard bay leaf; season beans with Adobo.
- Divide beans evenly among serving plates. Divide cooked rice evenly among plates alongside beans.

36. Easy Black Beans and Tomatoes

"A quick side dish to serve with fish tacos or grilled chicken; serve in small bowls or use slotted spoon to plate alongside fish tacos or grilled chicken."

Serving: 4 | Prep: 5 m | Cook: 10 m | Ready in: 15 m

Ingredients

- 1 (15 ounce) can black beans, rinsed and drained
- 1 (14.5 ounce) can no-salt-added diced tomatoes
- 1 small lime, juiced (optional)
- 1 teaspoon chili powder, or more to taste
- 1 teaspoon ground cumin, or more to taste
- 1 teaspoon garlic powder, or more to taste

Direction

- Stir black beans, tomatoes, lime juice, chili powder, cumin, and garlic powder together in a saucepan over medium heat; cook until the tomatoes soften, 10 to 15 minutes.

Nutrition Information

- Calories: 123 calories
- Total Fat: 0.7 g
- Cholesterol: 0 mg
- Sodium: 426 mg
- Total Carbohydrate: 23.6 g
- Protein: 7.5 g

37. Easy Chicken Fajita Soup

"This soup is simply made, with chicken, peppers, onions, and tomatoes in a delicious seasoned broth. Serve the soup as is or top with tortilla chips."

Serving: 10 | Prep: 20 m | Cook: 55 m | Ready in: 1 h 15 m

Ingredients

- 2 tablespoons vegetable oil
- 1 pound skinless, boneless chicken breasts, cut into strips
- 1 (1.27 ounce) packet fajita seasoning
- 1 red bell pepper, cut into thin strips
- 1 green bell pepper, cut into thin strips
- 1 poblano pepper, cut into thin strips
- 1 large onion, cut into thin strips
- 1 (14.5 ounce) can fire roasted diced tomatoes
- 1 (15 ounce) can seasoned black beans
- 1 (14 ounce) can chicken broth
- 1 dash hot sauce
- salt and pepper to taste

Direction

- Heat oil in a large soup pot over medium heat. Place chicken in the hot oil; cook, stirring only occasionally, until brown, about 10 minutes. Sprinkle fajita seasoning over the browned chicken and stir well to coat. Add the red and green bell pepper, poblano pepper, and onion to the seasoned chicken. Stir and cook over medium heat until the vegetables are soft, about 10 minutes.

- Pour the fire roasted tomatoes, black beans, and chicken broth into the pot with the chicken and vegetables. Bring the soup to a boil over high heat, then reduce the heat to medium-low, and simmer uncovered for 30 minutes, stirring occasionally.
- Season the soup with hot sauce, salt, and pepper to taste before serving.

Nutrition Information

- Calories: 143 calories
- Total Fat: 5.5 g
- Cholesterol: 24 mg
- Sodium: 714 mg
- Total Carbohydrate: 15.6 g
- Protein: 12.4 g

38. Easy Turkey Chili

"This chili is super quick to prepare, and is ready in less than an hour. Garnish with cheese."

Serving: 6 | Prep: 10 m | Cook: 45 m | Ready in: 55 m

Ingredients

- 1 teaspoon vegetable oil
- 1 pound ground turkey
- 1/2 onion, chopped
- 2 cups chicken broth
- 1 (28 ounce) can crushed tomatoes
- 1 (15 ounce) can black beans, rinsed and drained
- 1 (15 ounce) can kidney beans, rinsed and drained
- 1 (16 ounce) can refried beans
- 1 tablespoon minced garlic
- 2 1/2 tablespoons chili powder
- 1 teaspoon paprika
- 1 teaspoon dried oregano
- 1/2 teaspoon ground cumin
- salt and ground black pepper to taste
- 2 tablespoons shredded Cheddar cheese (optional)

Direction

- Heat vegetable oil in a large pot over medium-high heat and stir in the ground turkey. Cook and stir until the turkey is crumbly, evenly browned, and no longer pink. Drain and discard any excess grease. Stir in the onion; cook and stir until the onion is tender, about 5 minutes.

- Add the chicken broth, tomatoes, black beans, kidney beans, refried beans, garlic, chili powder, paprika, oregano, cumin, salt, and black pepper. Bring to a boil, then reduce heat to low. Cover and simmer for 30 minutes. Sprinkle each bowl with a teaspoon of Cheddar cheese, if desired.

Nutrition Information

- Calories: 299 calories
- Total Fat: 9.4 g
- Cholesterol: 65 mg
- Sodium: 655 mg
- Total Carbohydrate: 31.2 g
- Protein: 25.2 g

39. Enchilada Casserole

"The inclusion of tempeh adds a good measure of protein to this spicy enchilada casserole. You can replace the Cheddar cheese with Monterey Jack if you like. Serve with sour cream and salsa!"

Serving: 8 | Prep: 15 m | Cook: 45 m | Ready in: 1 h

Ingredients

- 1 (15 ounce) can black beans, rinsed and drained
- 2 cloves garlic, minced
- 1 onion, chopped
- 1 (4 ounce) can diced green chile peppers
- 1 jalapeno pepper, seeded and minced
- 1 (8 ounce) package tempeh, crumbled
- 6 (6 inch) corn tortillas
- 1 (19 ounce) can enchilada sauce
- 1 (6 ounce) can sliced black olives
- 8 ounces shredded Cheddar cheese

Direction

- Preheat oven to 350 degrees (175 degrees C). Lightly oil a 9x13 inch baking dish.
- In a medium bowl, combine the beans, garlic, onion, chile peppers, jalapeno pepper, and tempeh. Pour enchilada sauce into a shallow bowl.
- Dip three tortillas in the enchilada sauce, and place them in the prepared baking dish. Be sure to cover the bottom of the dish as completely as possible. Place 1/2 of the bean mixture on top

of the tortillas, and repeat. Drizzle the remaining sauce over the casserole, and sprinkle with olives and shredded cheese.
- Cover, and bake for 30 minutes. Uncover, and continue baking for an additional 15 minutes, or until the casserole is bubbling and the cheese is melted.

Nutrition Information

- Calories: 375 calories
- Total Fat: 24 g
- Cholesterol: 54 mg
- Sodium: 709 mg
- Total Carbohydrate: 24.9 g
- Protein: 17.4 g

40. Fiesta Chicken and Black Bean Enchiladas from Mission

"Shredded chicken, black beans, corn, cheese, and chiles in a creamy sauce are rolled into tortillas and baked with enchilada sauce and more cheese for this family-pleasing favorite."

Serving: 4 | Prep: 10 m | Cook: 1 h 10 m | Ready in: 1 h 20 m

Ingredients

- 8 Mission® Soft Taco Flour Tortillas
- Cooking spray
- 1/4 cup chicken broth
- 1 (16 ounce) skinless, boneless chicken breast
- 1 medium onion, diced
- 1 red pepper, stemmed, seeded, and diced
- 1 (15 ounce) can black beans, rinsed, drained
- 1 cup corn kernels
- 1/4 cup packed chopped fresh cilantro
- 1 (4 ounce) can diced green chiles
- 2 1/4 cups grated low-fat sharp Cheddar cheese, divided
- 2/3 cup fat-free sour cream
- 2/3 cup enchilada sauce
- Hot pepper sauce such as Tabasco®
- Salt and pepper to taste

Direction

- Heat oven to 350 degrees F. Spray an 8x11x2-inch baking dish with cooking spray.

- Pour chicken broth into a small frying pan, heat to simmer, add chicken breast, cover and simmer until no longer pink, turning once (approximately 25 minutes). Cool and shred.
- In same frying pan, add onions and red pepper. Sauté over medium heat until soft, approximately 5 minutes. Remove from heat.
- In a large bowl, place chicken, onion-pepper mixture, beans, corn, cilantro, chilies, 2 cups of the cheese, and sour cream. Toss until thoroughly blended. Add tabasco, salt and pepper to taste.
- Place 1/8 of mixture into center of each tortilla, roll and place in baking dish. When all 8 rolls are completed, pour Enchilada sauce over top and sprinkle with remaining 1/4 cup cheese. Bake for 35 minutes, or until sauce bubbles and enchiladas are heated through. Makes 4 generous servings of 2 enchiladas each.

Nutrition Information

- Calories: 724 calories
- Total Fat: 24.2 g
- Cholesterol: 112 mg
- Sodium: 2174 mg
- Total Carbohydrate: 92.8 g
- Protein: 57.9 g

41. Flaming Burritos

"Kids especially love these. They are delicious, fun to make, and require zero clean-up - the perfect camping food! This recipe is based on a tried-and-true Girl Scouts® tradition. Serve with salsa and sour cream on the side."

Serving: 4 | Prep: 20 m | Cook: 12 m | Ready in: 32 m

Ingredients

- 1 pound ground beef
- 1 (15 ounce) can black beans, drained and rinsed
- 1 large red bell pepper, chopped
- 4 (10 inch) flour tortillas
- 4 cups shredded mozzarella cheese, divided

Direction

- Heat a large nonstick skillet over medium heat. Add ground beef; cook and stir until browned, 5 to 10 minutes. Stir in black beans and red bell pepper; cook until heated through, about 5 minutes.
- Cut four 13x13-inch pieces of aluminum foil.
- Place 1 tortilla on each piece of aluminum foil. Spoon beef mixture in a line down the center of each tortilla. Divide cheese evenly among tortillas. Fold opposing edges of each tortilla to overlap the filling. Roll up in the shape of a burrito, sealing ends.
- Rinse and dry 4 half-gallon wax-lined milk cartons. Cut several 1-inch diamond-shaped vents into 2 corners of each milk carton, near the bottom. Place a wrapped burrito inside each carton.

- Place milk cartons in a safe cooking area outdoors. Light each on fire at one of the vents; cook until cartons burn down, about 2 minutes. Gently unwrap burritos with heatproof gloves.

Nutrition Information

- Calories: 820 calories
- Total Fat: 37.5 g
- Cholesterol: 143 mg
- Sodium: 1620 mg
- Total Carbohydrate: 59.1 g
- Protein: 59.1 g

42. Goya Black Bean Salsa

"An addictive black bean corn salsa--Here's the black bean salsa you've been looking for. You know how to make salsa the traditional way--now, try our black bean corn salsa for a fun surprise at parties or at home. Spice things up even more with GOYA® Pickled Jalapenos and GOYA® Chili Powder. This zesty black bean salsa recipe is perfect as a dip, served with tortilla chips, or used to top nachos and tacos."

Serving: 8 | Prep: 5 m | Ready in: 5 m

Ingredients

- 2 (15.5 ounce) cans Goya Black Beans, drained and rinsed
- 1 (17.6 ounce) container Goya Salsa Pico de Gallo
- 1 (15.25 ounce) can Goya Whole Kernel Corn, drained
- 3 tablespoons Goya Extra Virgin Olive Oil
- Goya Green Pickled Jalapeno Nacho Slices (optional)
- 1 tablespoon Goya Chili Powder
- 2 teaspoons Goya Cumin
- 2 teaspoons Goya Minced Garlic

Direction

- In large bowl, combine all ingredients. Using large spoon, gently mix to combine. Serve with tortilla chips. Or, cover bowl with plastic wrap and refrigerate until ready to eat.

43. Grillable Vegan Burger

"This vegan burger recipe can be made ahead of time and frozen for later, or quickly whipped up for a barbeque when needed. It's absolutely delicious!"

Serving: 10 | Prep: 25 m | Cook: 10 m | Ready in: 35 m

Ingredients

- 2 cups raw walnuts
- 2 tablespoons olive oil
- 1 onion, minced
- salt and ground black pepper to taste
- 3 cups rinsed and drained canned black beans
- 2 cups cooked rice
- 3/4 cup barbeque sauce
- 2/3 cup cornflake crumbs
- 2 tablespoons brown sugar
- 2 tablespoons chile powder
- 2 tablespoons ground paprika
- 2 tablespoons ground cumin

Direction

- Toast walnuts in a skillet over medium heat, stirring frequently until lightly browned and fragrant, 5 to 7 minutes. Crush into fine pieces using a mortar and pestle or food processor.
- Heat olive oil in the same skillet over medium heat. Cook and stir onion until lightly browned, about 5 minutes. Season with salt and pepper.
- Mash black beans in a large bowl using a fork. Add walnuts, onion, rice, barbeque sauce, cornflake crumbs, brown sugar,

chile powder, paprika, and cumin. Season with salt and pepper; stir until mixture is well combined and holds together.
- Shape mixture into 10 patties.

Nutrition Information

- Calories: 445 calories
- Total Fat: 19.6 g
- Cholesterol: 0 mg
- Sodium: 726 mg
- Total Carbohydrate: 58.7 g
- Protein: 11.6 g

44. Hash Brown Tostadas

"This Hash Brown Tostadas recipe is courtesy of A Communal Table, a part of the U.S. Potato Board's Potato Lovers Club Program."

Serving: 4 | Prep: 30 m | Cook: 1 h | Ready in: 1 h 30 m

Ingredients

- 4 cups frozen shredded hash brown potatoes
- 6 tablespoons vegetable oil, divided
- 1 (15 ounce) can reduced-sodium black beans, rinsed and drained
- 1 bunch cilantro
- 1 lime, juiced
- 1 teaspoon cumin
- 1/2 teaspoon garlic paste
- 1/4 teaspoon cayenne pepper
- 1 teaspoon salt
- 2 cups romaine salad blend
- 1 cup fresh tomato salsa
- 1 cup shredded Mexican cheese blend
- Avocado (optional)
- Green onions (optional)
- Low-fat sour cream (optional)

Direction

- Place shredded potatoes in a microwave-safe bowl and microwave for 3 minutes. While potatoes are heating, pour 3 tablespoons vegetable oil into a 12-inch cast-iron or nonstick skillet. Heat the oil over medium to medium-high heat.

- Remove the potatoes from the microwave and spoon 1 cup of the potatoes into the skillet. Repeat with another cup of potatoes and flatten each mound of potatoes to make a patty. Cook hash browns for 5 minutes.
- While hash browns are cooking, drain and rinse the beans. Combine beans with a large handful of cilantro, lime juice, cumin, garlic paste, cayenne, and salt in the bowl of a mini food processor. Process until smooth. Set aside.
- Turn the potato patties over and cook for another 5 minutes, until they are lightly browned. Dice the avocado and slice the green onions.
- Remove the patties from the pan. Add the remaining 3 tablespoons oil to the pan and repeat with the remaining potatoes.
- Spread 2 tablespoons of the black bean mixture on each patty and top with romaine, salsa, cheese, avocado, green onions and sour cream (if using).

Nutrition Information

- Calories: 487 calories
- Total Fat: 38.3 g
- Cholesterol: 33 mg
- Sodium: 1506 mg
- Total Carbohydrate: 40.1 g
- Protein: 15.6 g

45. Hearty Ham Bone Black Bean Soup

"The best black bean soup! If you are looking for a recipe for a hearty, low-fat soup using a leftover ham bone, this is for you! Key is discarding thick fat from the soup and you must use green chiles. Enjoy!"

Serving: 4 | Prep: 10 m | Cook: 5 h 51 m | Ready in: 14 h 1 m

Ingredients

- 1 ham bone with some meat
- 1 drizzle olive oil
- 3 stalks celery with leaves, chopped, or more to taste
- 1/2 onion, chopped
- 4 cloves garlic, crushed
- 1/2 (12 ounce) package baby carrots
- 1 cup fingerling potatoes, or to taste
- 1 small red bell pepper, seeded and chopped (optional)
- 4 cups water
- 1 (19 ounce) can black beans, drained and rinsed
- 1 (12 fluid ounce) can vegetable juice (such as V8®)
- 1 (11 ounce) can canned corn (such as Green Giant Niblets®), drained (optional)
- 2 tomatoes, chopped
- 2 tablespoons chopped green chilies
- 2 teaspoons ground cumin
- salt and ground black pepper to taste

Direction

- Place ham bone in a large slow cooker.

- Heat olive oil in a large saucepan over medium-high heat. Sauté celery, onion, and garlic until onion is translucent, about 5 minutes. Pour mixture over the ham bone in the slow cooker.
- Sauté carrots, potatoes, and red bell pepper in the same saucepan until coated in oil, about 1 minute. Transfer vegetables to the slow cooker; add water, black beans, vegetable juice, corn, tomatoes, green chiles, cumin, salt, and black pepper. Cover and cook on High until soup is warm, 45 minutes to 1 hour. Reduce heat to Low; continue to cook for 5 to 6 hours.
- Remove ham bone from the soup. Separate meat from the bone and return to the soup; discard the bone. Cover soup and refrigerate, 8 hours to overnight. Discard thick fat on the top of the soup and reheat.

Nutrition Information

- Calories: 310 calories
- Total Fat: 2.3 g
- Cholesterol: 0 mg
- Sodium: 1140 mg
- Total Carbohydrate: 60.8 g
- Protein: 13.5 g

46. Herbed Rice and Spicy Black Bean Salad

"Delicious fresh herbs and a blend of peppers make this a fresh, light, and healthy dish that can be a side or a main course. My family loves this on warm summer nights."

Serving: 8 | Prep: 45 m | Ready in: 55 m

Ingredients

- 1 tablespoon chopped fresh basil
- 1 tablespoon chopped fresh thyme
- 1 tablespoon chopped fresh parsley
- 1 tablespoon chopped fresh cilantro
- 1/2 teaspoon salt
- 1/2 teaspoon ground black pepper
- 1/2 teaspoon cayenne pepper
- 1/4 teaspoon garlic powder
- 2 cups cold, cooked white rice
- 1 (14 ounce) can black beans, rinsed and drained
- 2 celery stalks, finely chopped
- 1 (4 ounce) can chopped black olives
- 3 green onions, chopped
- 1/4 cup red wine vinegar
- 1/4 cup extra-virgin olive oil

Direction

- Make a seasoning by mixing together the basil, thyme, parsley, cilantro, salt, pepper, cayenne pepper, and garlic powder in a bowl.

- Gently mix together the rice, black beans, celery, olives, and green onions in a large bowl. Season the rice mixture with 1 teaspoon of the seasoning.
- Make a dressing by whisking the vinegar and olive oil with the seasoning; allow to rest for 10 minutes. Pour the dressing over the rice mixture; stir to combine.

Nutrition Information

- Calories: 185 calories
- Total Fat: 8.8 g
- Cholesterol: 0 mg
- Sodium: 477 mg
- Total Carbohydrate: 22.1 g
- Protein: 4.5 g

47. Hispanic Tilapia and Rice Bowl

"A quick and easy dish that comes alive on those busy days."

Serving: 4 | Prep: 5 m | Cook: 20 m | Ready in: 25 m

Ingredients

- 4 (4 ounce) tilapia fillets
- 1 tablespoon vegetable oil
- 1 (15 ounce) can reduced-sodium black beans, rinsed and drained
- 1 (15.25 ounce) can no-salt-added whole-kernel corn, drained
- 1 3/4 cups water
- 2 tablespoons medium chunky salsa
- 1/4 teaspoon cumin
- 1/4 teaspoon chili powder
- 1 (5.4 ounce) package Knorr® Fiesta Sides™ - Yellow Rice
- Salt and pepper to taste

Direction

- Pat tilapia filets dry with paper towels and season both sides with salt and pepper.
- In large skillet, heat oil and add tilapia filets. Cook until fish releases easily with a spatula; flip and cook until fish is cooked through and flakes easily with a fork, 5 to 8 minutes. Remove from skillet and set aside, tenting loosely with foil to keep warm.
- Add beans, corn, water, salsa, cumin, chili powder and contents of rice package to skillet, stir well. Bring to a boil,

cover and reduce heat. Simmer until water has been absorbed and rice is tender, about 7 minutes.
- Place rice in a serving dish and top with fish. Serve immediately.

Nutrition Information

- Calories: 461 calories
- Total Fat: 6.1 g
- Cholesterol: 41 mg
- Sodium: 550 mg
- Total Carbohydrate: 61.5 g
- Protein: 34.5 g

48. Instant Pot Vegan 15Bean Soup

"This vegan version of the traditional 15-bean soup is the perfect comfort food. Hearty and rich, this tasty soup is so easy to make in your Instant Pot®."

Serving: 6 | Prep: 10 m | Cook: 45 m | Ready in: 1 h 10 m

Ingredients

- 1 (20 ounce) package 15-bean soup mix (seasoning packet not used)
- 1 (14.5 ounce) can diced Italian-style tomatoes
- 8 cups vegetable broth
- 2 carrots, diced
- 1 onion, diced
- 2 stalks celery, chopped
- 2 cloves garlic, minced
- 1 teaspoon sea salt
- 1 teaspoon smoked paprika
- 1/2 teaspoon ground black pepper

Direction

- Combine rinsed beans, diced tomatoes, vegetable broth, carrots, onion, celery, garlic, salt, paprika, and black pepper in a multi-functional pressure cooker (such as Instant Pot(R)). Close and lock the lid. Select high pressure according to manufacturer's instructions; set timer for 35 minutes. Allow 10 to 15 minutes for pressure to build.

- Release pressure using the natural-release method according to manufacturer's instructions, about 10 minutes. Complete releasing pressure carefully using the quick-release method according to manufacturer's instructions, about 5 minutes. Unlock and remove the lid.

Nutrition Information

- Calories: 390 calories
- Total Fat: 2.2 g
- Cholesterol: 0 mg
- Sodium: 1214 mg
- Total Carbohydrate: 67 g
- Protein: 23.6 g

49. Jennifers Corn Salad

"I had this on the fourth of July for the first time. It's my cousin's recipe. I almost ate the whole bowl. So light and fresh. Serve with chips. Tostitos® Scoops!® work great!"

Serving: 6 | Prep: 10 m | Ready in: 40 m

Ingredients

- 1 (15 ounce) can black beans, rinsed and drained
- 1 (11 ounce) can shoepeg corn, drained
- 1 (8 ounce) package crumbled feta cheese
- 4 green onions, chopped
- 1/4 cup olive oil
- 1/4 cup cider vinegar
- 2 tablespoons white sugar

Direction

- Mix black beans, corn, feta cheese, and green onions together in a bowl.
- Whisk olive oil, vinegar, and sugar together in a separate bowl until smooth; drizzle over corn mixture and toss to coat.
- Cover bowl with plastic wrap and refrigerate until flavors blend, at least 30 minutes.

Nutrition Information

- Calories: 321 calories
- Total Fat: 17.8 g
- Cholesterol: 34 mg

- Sodium: 845 mg
- Total Carbohydrate: 29.1 g
- Protein: 11.2 g

50. Kellys Black Bean Salad

"My sister Kelly makes this AMAZING salad anytime we have a family get-together. It is loved by everyone in the family. The Mexican flavor is is unbeatable! Keeps in the fridge for up to a week!"

Serving: 10 | Prep: 15 m | Cook: 20 m | Ready in: 35 m

Ingredients

- 1 cup white rice
- 2 cups water
- 1 (14.5 ounce) can diced tomatoes, drained
- 1/3 cup red wine vinegar
- 3 cloves garlic, minced
- 1 tablespoon ground cumin
- 4 teaspoons chili powder
- 1 1/2 teaspoons salt
- 1 teaspoon oregano
- ground black pepper to taste
- 3/4 cup canola oil
- 3 (15.5 ounce) cans black beans, drained and rinsed
- 1/2 (10 ounce) box frozen corn, thawed

Direction

- Bring rice and water to a boil in a saucepan. Reduce heat to medium-low, cover, and simmer until rice is tender and the liquid has been absorbed, 20 to 25 minutes.
- Mix tomatoes, vinegar, garlic, cumin, chili powder, salt, oregano, and black pepper together in a bowl. Whisk oil into tomato mixture to make a dressing.

- Stir rice, black beans, and corn together in a bowl; toss with dressing until well-coated.

Nutrition Information

- Calories: 374 calories
- Total Fat: 17.8 g
- Cholesterol: 0 mg
- Sodium: 926 mg
- Total Carbohydrate: 45 g
- Protein: 10.4 g

51. Leftover Salmon Lunch Wrap

"I am currently eating clean so I needed a quick and healthy lunch recipe. I already had pepper slices and leftover salmon in the refrigerator so I just decided to throw something together! This recipe is fresh and delicious and easily doubled for multiple people."

Serving: 2 | Prep: 15 m | Cook: 11 m | Ready in: 26 m

Ingredients

- 1 (15 ounce) can black beans, drained
- 1 (3 ounce) fillet cooked salmon
- 2 (6 inch) flour tortillas
- 1 red bell pepper, thinly sliced
- 1 green bell pepper, thinly sliced
- 1 small avocado, halved and sliced

Direction

- Heat black beans in a small saucepan over medium-low heat until warmed through, about 5 minutes.
- Reheat salmon in a covered skillet over medium-low heat, 3 to 5 minutes per side. Slice into smaller pieces.
- Divide black beans and salmon evenly between the tortillas. Cover with red bell pepper, green bell pepper, and avocado slices. Wrap up tortillas.

Nutrition Information

- Calories: 519 calories
- Total Fat: 17.7 g

- Cholesterol: 23 mg
- Sodium: 1054 mg
- Total Carbohydrate: 65.2 g
- Protein: 28.2 g

52. LowCarb GlutenFree Black Bean and Lentil Burgers

"Low-carb, low-fat, gluten-free, and vegetarian burgers. Serve on buns or just by themselves."

Serving: 8 | Prep: 30 m | Cook: 25 m | Ready in: 1 h 25 m

Ingredients

- 1 (14 ounce) can black beans, rinsed and drained
- 1 medium onion, finely chopped
- 1 bell pepper, finely chopped
- 1/2 cup finely chopped mushrooms
- 1 jalapeno pepper, finely chopped (optional)
- 2 cloves garlic, minced
- salt and ground black pepper to taste
- 1 tablespoon olive oil
- 3/4 cup ground lentils, or as needed
- 1 egg
- 2 tablespoons ground cumin
- 1 tablespoon chili powder
- 1/2 teaspoon smoked paprika

Direction

- Mash black beans with a fork until chunky but not totally smooth.
- Combine onion, bell pepper, mushrooms, jalapeno pepper, and garlic in a bowl. Season with salt and pepper.

- Heat olive oil in a large skillet over medium heat. Sauté vegetable mixture until softened, 5 to 8 minutes. Season with salt and pepper.
- Transfer vegetable mixture to a food processor; pulse for 1 to 2 minutes. Mix into black beans. Mix in ground lentils and egg. Add cumin, chili powder, and paprika. Refrigerate mixture for 30 minutes.
- Preheat the oven to 375 degrees F (190 degrees C). Line a baking sheet with parchment paper.
- Shape cooled mixture into patties. Arrange on the baking sheet.
- Bake until browned, 10 to 15 minutes per side.

Nutrition Information

- Calories: 154 calories
- Total Fat: 3.2 g
- Cholesterol: 20 mg
- Sodium: 233 mg
- Total Carbohydrate: 23.3 g
- Protein: 9.4 g

53. Mexican Bean and Rice Salad

"Quick, fresh and tasty. I love the ingredients of this recipe."

Serving: 10 | Prep: 20 m | Ready in: 1 h 20 m

Ingredients

- 2 cups cooked brown rice
- 1 (15 ounce) can kidney beans, rinsed and drained
- 1 (15 ounce) can black beans, rinsed and drained
- 1 (15.25 ounce) can whole kernel corn, drained
- 1 small onion, diced
- 1 green bell pepper, diced
- 2 jalapeno peppers, seeded and diced
- 1 lime, zested and juiced
- 1/4 cup chopped cilantro leaves
- 1 teaspoon minced garlic
- 1 1/2 teaspoons ground cumin
- salt to taste

Direction

- In a large salad bowl, combine the brown rice, kidney beans, black beans, corn, onion, green pepper, jalapeno peppers, lime zest and juice, cilantro, garlic, and cumin. Lightly toss all ingredients to mix well, and sprinkle with salt to taste.
- Refrigerate salad for 1 hour, toss again, and serve.

Nutrition Information

- Calories: 124 calories
- Total Fat: 1 g
- Cholesterol: 0 mg
- Sodium: 220 mg
- Total Carbohydrate: 26 g
- Protein: 4.7 g

54. Mexican Casserole

"Chicken breast simmered with a spicy black bean and corn mixture, then topped with cheese and tortilla chip crumbs and baked. Easy and quick to fix weekday casserole with a Mexican flair. Nutritious and kid friendly."

Serving: 5 | Prep: 15 m | Cook: 15 m | Ready in: 30 m

Ingredients

- 2 tablespoons vegetable oil
- 3/4 pound cubed skinless, boneless chicken breast meat
- 1/2 (1.25 ounce) package taco seasoning mix
- 1 (15 ounce) can black beans, rinsed and drained
- 1 (8.75 ounce) can sweet corn, drained
- 1/4 cup salsa
- water as needed
- 1 cup shredded Mexican-style cheese
- 1 1/2 cups crushed plain tortilla chips

Direction

- In a large skillet over medium high heat, sauté chicken in oil until cooked through and no longer pink inside. Add taco seasoning, beans, corn, salsa and a little water to prevent drying out. Cover skillet and simmer over medium low heat for 10 minutes.
- Preheat oven to 350 degrees F (175 degrees C).
- Transfer chicken mixture to a 9x13 inch baking dish. Top with 1/2 cup of the cheese and crushed tortilla chips.
- Bake in the preheated oven for 15 minutes. Add remaining 1/2 cup cheese and bake until cheese is melted and bubbly.

Nutrition Information

- Calories: 384 calories
- Total Fat: 16.6 g
- Cholesterol: 59 mg
- Sodium: 1286 mg
- Total Carbohydrate: 34 g
- Protein: 26.8 g

55. Mexican Fiesta with Sorghum Grain

"Go south of the border! Fresh veggies, shredded chicken and sorghum create a festive meal or snack your friends and family will devour. Add sour cream and salsa to make it a party for your taste buds."

Serving: 4 | Prep: 20 m | Ready in: 20 m

Ingredients

- 1 cup whole grain sorghum, uncooked
- 4 cups water
- 2 cups cooked, shredded chicken
- 1 tablespoon Mexican seasoning blend
- 1 avocado, halved and sliced
- 1 cup pico de gallo
- 1 cup roasted corn salsa
- 1 cup black beans
- Lime wedges
- Sour cream

Direction

- In a small saucepan, boil 4 cups of water and add 1 cup of whole grain sorghum to make 3 cups of cooked sorghum. Cover with a tight-fitting lid, reduce heat to medium and simmer for 45 minutes or until tender. Fluff with a fork.
- In a large bowl combine chicken and Mexican seasoning. Add in the cooked sorghum, avocado, pico de gallo, corn salsa, and black beans. Season to taste with salt and pepper. Serve with lime wedges and sour cream.

Nutrition Information

- Calories: 565 calories
- Total Fat: 10.2 g
- Cholesterol: 59 mg
- Sodium: 755 mg
- Total Carbohydrate: 81.2 g
- Protein: 35.1 g

56. Mexicorn

"This is a bright, colorful salad that anyone could love."

Serving: 7 | Prep: 20 m | Ready in: 20 m

Ingredients

- 3 (15 ounce) cans black beans, rinsed and drained
- 3 (15.25 ounce) cans whole kernel corn, drained
- 1/2 red onion, diced
- 2 green bell peppers, diced
- 1 (7 ounce) jar roasted red peppers, drained and diced
- 1/3 cup red wine vinegar
- 1/3 cup canola oil

Direction

- Into a large bowl, mix together the beans, corn, red onion, green pepper and red pepper.
- Right before serving, pour enough red wine vinegar over all to coat. Add just enough oil to make it shiny.

Nutrition Information

- Calories: 261 calories
- Total Fat: 12.5 g
- Cholesterol: 0 mg
- Sodium: 930 mg
- Total Carbohydrate: 38.6 g
- Protein: 5.4 g

57. Old Mamas Fashioned Chili

"This spooky chili is great for Halloween dinner! Keep warm on the stove and the little ones can eat anytime during trick-or-treat activities."

Serving: 8 | Prep: 15 m | Cook: 25 m | Ready in: 40 m

Ingredients

- 1 pound ground beef
- 2 (15 ounce) cans black beans, undrained
- 2 (15 ounce) cans kidney beans, undrained
- 2 (14.5 ounce) cans stewed tomatoes, undrained
- 2 green bell peppers, cut into 1/2-inch dice
- 1 yellow onion, cut into 1/2-inch dice
- 4 cloves garlic, minced
- 1 (1.25 ounce) package chili seasoning mix, or to taste
- 1 dash hot sauce, or to taste
- salt and ground black pepper to taste

Direction

- Cook and stir ground beef in a skillet over medium-high heat until crumbly and browned, 5 to 10 minutes. Drain.
- Stir drained ground beef, black beans, kidney beans, tomatoes, green bell peppers, yellow onion, garlic, and chili seasoning together in a large pot over medium-high heat. Bring to a boil, reduce heat to low, and simmer, stirring occasionally, until vegetables are slightly tender and chili is heated through, 15 to 20 minutes. Season with hot sauce, salt, and ground black pepper to taste.

Nutrition Information

- Calories: 362 calories
- Total Fat: 10.2 g
- Cholesterol: 35 mg
- Sodium: 1313 mg
- Total Carbohydrate: 46.7 g
- Protein: 23.7 g

58. Pacific Cuban Black Beans and Rice

"I am not claiming this to be an authentic Cuban dish, rather my version of it. I hope that you enjoy. Garnish with chopped green onions, chopped cilantro, lime wedges, and sour cream."

Serving: 6 | Prep: 20 m | Cook: 1 h 15 m | Ready in: 1 h 35 m

Ingredients

- 4 cups water
- 2 cups rice
- 3 tablespoons olive oil
- 1 onion, chopped
- 1 bell pepper, chopped
- 2 carrots, peeled and chopped
- 2 ribs celery, chopped
- 1 tablespoon minced garlic
- 2 (15 ounce) cans black beans
- 2 smoked Spanish chorizo sausage links, coarsely chopped
- 1 cup chicken stock
- 1 (8 ounce) jar picante sauce
- 2 bay leaves
- 2 teaspoons smoked paprika
- 1 teaspoon red wine vinegar, or more to taste
- 1 teaspoon ground cumin
- 1 teaspoon white sugar
- 1 teaspoon salt, or to taste
- 1/2 teaspoon ground black pepper, or to taste
- 1 pinch red pepper flakes (optional)

Direction

- Bring water and rice to a boil in a saucepan. Reduce heat to medium-low, cover, and simmer until the rice is tender and liquid has been absorbed, 20 to 25 minutes.
- Heat olive oil in a stockpot over medium-high heat; sauté onion, bell pepper, carrots, celery, and garlic in hot oil until tender, about 5 minutes.
- Mix black beans with liquid, chorizo, chicken stock, picante sauce, bay leaves, paprika, red wine vinegar, cumin, sugar, salt, black pepper, and red pepper flakes together in the pot with the onion mixture; bring to a boil, reduce heat to medium-low, place a cover on the pot, and simmer until the beans have softened, about 30 minutes.
- Remove lid from pot and continue cooking until the mixture reaches your desired consistency, at least 20 minutes more. Remove bay leaves and adjust seasoning to your preferences. Serve over rice.

Nutrition Information

- Calories: 559 calories
- Total Fat: 15.8 g
- Cholesterol: 18 mg
- Sodium: 1609 mg
- Total Carbohydrate: 84.5 g
- Protein: 19.6 g

59. PAMs Spicy Slow Cooker Chicken Tortilla Soup

"A slow cooker chicken tortilla soup recipe with chicken thighs, Southwest mixed vegetables, zesty tomatoes, spices and fresh lime juice."

Serving: 6 | Prep: 15 m | Ready in: 8 h 15 m

Ingredients

- PAM® Original No-Stick Cooking Spray
- 1 1/2 pounds boneless skinless chicken thighs
- 2 cups frozen Southwest mixed vegetables (corn, black beans, red peppers)
- 1 (10 ounce) can Ro*Tel® Original Diced Tomatoes Green Chilies, undrained
- 1 tablespoon ground chipotle chili pepper
- 1 1/2 teaspoons ground cumin
- 4 cups chicken broth
- 1/4 cup fresh lime juice
- Tortilla strips (optional)
- Diced avocado (optional)
- Chopped cilantro (optional)

Direction

- Spray inside of 4-quart slow cooker with cooking spray. Place chicken, frozen vegetables, undrained tomatoes, chili pepper, cumin and broth in slow cooker.
- Cover; cook on LOW 6 to 8 hours or until chicken is tender. Remove chicken from slow cooker; pull into shreds with 2 forks.

Return chicken to slow cooker. Stir in lime juice. Serve and top with tortilla strips, avocado and cilantro, if desired.

Nutrition Information

- Calories: 269 calories
- Total Fat: 12.5 g
- Cholesterol: 67 mg
- Sodium: 893 mg
- Total Carbohydrate: 15.9 g
- Protein: 22.2 g

60. Pumpkin Black Bean Soup

"This is a delicious soup that is even better reheated the next day. Easy to make too. Serve with a garnish of sour cream and toasted pumpkin seeds if desired."

Serving: 9 | Prep: 15 m | Cook: 30 m | Ready in: 45 m

Ingredients

- 3 (15 ounce) cans black beans, rinsed and drained
- 1 (16 ounce) can diced tomatoes
- 1/4 cup butter
- 1 1/4 cups chopped onion
- 4 cloves garlic, chopped
- 1 teaspoon salt
- 1/2 teaspoon ground black pepper
- 4 cups beef broth
- 1 (15 ounce) can pumpkin puree
- 1/2 pound cubed cooked ham
- 3 tablespoons sherry vinegar

Direction

- Pour 2 cans of the black beans into a food processor or blender, along with the can of tomatoes. Puree until smooth. Set aside.
- Melt butter in a soup pot over medium heat. Add the onion and garlic, and season with salt and pepper. Cook and stir until the onion is softened. Stir in the bean puree, remaining can of beans, beef broth, pumpkin puree, and sherry vinegar. Mix until well blended, then simmer for about 25 minutes, or until thick

enough to coat the back of a metal spoon. Stir in the ham, and heat through before serving.

Nutrition Information

- Calories: 151 calories
- Total Fat: 10.2 g
- Cholesterol: 28 mg
- Sodium: 1052 mg
- Total Carbohydrate: 7.4 g
- Protein: 7.4 g

61. Quick and Easy Edamame Salad

"This salad is high in protein and healthy. A great side dish or stand-alone as a healthy lunch to bring to work.

Sesame-ginger dressing is available at most supermarkets and Japanese restaurants."

Serving: 8 | Prep: 15 m | Ready in: 15 m

Ingredients

- 3 cups hulled edamame
- 1 (15.5 ounce) can black beans, rinsed and drained
- 3/4 cup frozen corn, thawed
- 1/2 cup diced red onion
- 1/2 cup diced red bell pepper
- 2 tablespoons ginger sesame dressing, or to taste
- 2 teaspoons salt

Direction

- Combine edamame, black beans, corn, red onion, red pepper, ginger sesame dressing, and salt in a bowl; stir until well mixed. Place in the refrigerator until ready to serve.

Nutrition Information

- Calories: 230 calories
- Total Fat: 8.8 g

- Cholesterol: 0 mg
- Sodium: 852 mg
- Total Carbohydrate: 24.8 g
- Protein: 16.4 g

62. Quick and Easy Mexican Breakfast Tacos

"This quick and easy meal makes a great (vegetarian) breakfast or lunch!"

Serving: 4 | Prep: 15 m | Cook: 11 m | Ready in: 26 m

Ingredients

- cooking spray
- 4 eggs
- 1/2 cup frozen chopped spinach, thawed and drained
- 2 green onions, diced
- 1/8 teaspoon garlic salt
- 1/8 teaspoon Cajun seasoning
- 1 (15 ounce) can black beans, rinsed and drained
- 1 cup shredded Mexican cheese blend
- 4 (9 inch) tortillas whole wheat tortillas
- 2 tablespoons salsa
- 2 tablespoons fat-free sour cream

Direction

- Spray a large skillet with cooking spray; warm over medium-high heat. Whisk eggs together in a bowl. Pour into the skillet. Add spinach, green onions, garlic salt, and Cajun seasoning. Cook and stir until eggs are nearly set, about 5 minutes.
- Pour black beans into a small pot over medium heat. Cook, stirring occasionally, until heated through, about 5 minutes.
- Sprinkle Mexican cheese blend over tortillas. Place tortillas on microwave-safe plates or paper towels. Microwave 2 tortillas at

a time, about 30 minute seconds. Repeat with remaining tortillas.
- Divide egg mixture and beans over the center of the tortillas. Top with salsa and sour cream.

Nutrition Information

- Calories: 436 calories
- Total Fat: 17 g
- Cholesterol: 220 mg
- Sodium: 1168 mg
- Total Carbohydrate: 55.1 g
- Protein: 26.6 g

63. Quinoa and Black Bean Chili

"Vegetarian chili with quinoa. Sprinkle cheese on top to serve."

Serving: 10 | Prep: 30 m | Cook: 30 m | Ready in: 1 h

Ingredients

- 1 cup uncooked quinoa, rinsed
- 2 cups water
- 1 tablespoon vegetable oil
- 1 onion, chopped
- 4 cloves garlic, chopped
- 1 tablespoon chili powder
- 1 tablespoon ground cumin
- 1 (28 ounce) can crushed tomatoes
- 2 (19 ounce) cans black beans, rinsed and drained
- 1 green bell pepper, chopped
- 1 red bell pepper, chopped
- 1 zucchini, chopped
- 1 jalapeno pepper, seeded and minced
- 1 tablespoon minced chipotle peppers in adobo sauce
- 1 teaspoon dried oregano
- salt and ground black pepper to taste
- 1 cup frozen corn
- 1/4 cup chopped fresh cilantro

Direction

- Bring the quinoa and water to a boil in a saucepan over high heat. Reduce heat to medium-low, cover, and simmer until the

- quinoa is tender, and the water has been absorbed, about 15 to 20 minutes; set aside.
- Meanwhile, heat the vegetable oil in a large pot over medium heat. Stir in the onion, and cook until the onion softens and turns translucent, about 5 minutes. Add the garlic, chili powder, and cumin; cook and stir 1 minute to release the flavors. Stir in the tomatoes, black beans, green bell pepper, red bell pepper, zucchini, jalapeno pepper, chipotle pepper, and oregano. Season to taste with salt and pepper. Bring to a simmer over high heat, then reduce heat to medium-low, cover, and simmer 20 minutes.
- After 20 minutes, stir in the reserved quinoa and corn. Cook to reheat the corn for 5 minutes. Remove from the heat, and stir in the cilantro to serve.

Nutrition Information

- Calories: 233 calories
- Total Fat: 3.5 g
- Cholesterol: 0 mg
- Sodium: 540 mg
- Total Carbohydrate: 42 g
- Protein: 11.5 g

64. Quinoa Bean and Ground Turkey Chili

"Ground turkey chili with quinoa is great for chili dogs, nachos, or just in a bowl."

Serving: 8 | Prep: 15 m | Cook: 51 m | Ready in: 1 h 6 m

Ingredients

- 1 tablespoon ghee
- 1 pound ground turkey
- 1 large onion, chopped
- 5 cloves garlic, minced
- 1/4 teaspoon ground black pepper
- 1 (15 ounce) can diced tomatoes
- 1 (6 ounce) can tomato paste
- 2 stalks celery, chopped
- 2 tablespoons chili powder, or more to taste
- 1 tablespoon Worcestershire sauce
- 1 tablespoon ground cumin
- 1 teaspoon dried oregano
- 1/8 teaspoon garlic powder
- 1/8 teaspoon onion powder
- Himalayan pink salt to taste
- 4 cups vegetable broth
- 1 (15 ounce) can black beans, drained and rinsed
- 1 (15 ounce) can kidney beans, drained and rinsed
- 1 cup tri-colored quinoa

Direction

- Heat ghee in a Dutch oven over medium heat. Add turkey, onion, garlic, and black pepper. Cook and stir until turkey is browned, about 6 minutes. Drain and discard fat.
- Stir tomatoes, tomato paste, celery, chili powder, Worcestershire sauce, cumin, oregano, garlic powder, onion powder, and salt into the turkey mixture. Add broth, black beans, and kidney beans; stir to combine. Add quinoa; bring to a boil. Reduce heat to low and simmer until quinoa is tender, about 40 minutes.

Nutrition Information

- Calories: 335 calories
- Total Fat: 8.4 g
- Cholesterol: 46 mg
- Sodium: 889 mg
- Total Carbohydrate: 43.5 g
- Protein: 22.9 g

65. Quinoa Black Bean Burgers

"These vegetarian burgers are delicious! Your carnivorous friends will be impressed. My favorite way to serve is on a whole-wheat bun with garlic-lemon mayonnaise, fresh raw spinach, sliced tomato, and caramelized onions!"

Serving: 5 | Prep: 15 m | Cook: 20 m | Ready in: 35 m

Ingredients

- 1 (15 ounce) can black beans, rinsed and drained
- 1/4 cup quinoa
- 1/2 cup water
- 1/2 cup bread crumbs
- 1/4 cup minced yellow bell pepper
- 2 tablespoons minced onion
- 1 large clove garlic, minced
- 1 1/2 teaspoons ground cumin
- 1/2 teaspoon salt
- 1 teaspoon hot pepper sauce (such as Frank's RedHot®)
- 1 egg
- 3 tablespoons olive oil

Direction

- Bring the quinoa and water to a boil in a saucepan. Reduce heat to medium-low, cover, and simmer until the quinoa is tender and the water has been absorbed, about 15 to 20 minutes.
- Roughly mash the black beans with a fork leaving some whole black beans in a paste-like mixture.

- Mix the quinoa, bread crumbs, bell pepper, onion, garlic, cumin, salt, hot pepper sauce, and egg into the black beans using your hands.
- Form the black bean mixture into 5 patties.
- Heat the olive oil in a large skillet.
- Cook the patties in the hot oil until heated through, 2 to 3 minutes per side.

Nutrition Information

- Calories: 245 calories
- Total Fat: 10.6 g
- Cholesterol: 37 mg
- Sodium: 679 mg
- Total Carbohydrate: 28.9 g
- Protein: 9.3 g

66. Race Day Salsa

"Extremely fresh and crunchy, not your typical salsa! This is my husband's special treat for NASCAR Race Days. Can be frozen for up to 3 months with some loss of texture."

Serving: 10 | Prep: 15 m | Cook: 20 m | Ready in: 35 m

Ingredients

- 4 ears corn on the cob with husks
- 2 (15 ounce) cans no-salt-added black beans, drained and rinsed
- 6 Roma (plum) tomatoes, chopped
- 1 green bell pepper, chopped
- 1 red onion, diced
- 2 jalapeno peppers, chopped
- 1 lime, juiced
- 2 teaspoons chopped fresh cilantro
- 2 cloves garlic, minced
- 1 (12 fluid ounce) can tomato juice
- 1 (14 ounce) can tomato sauce
- 1 pinch kosher salt, or to taste
- 1 pinch ground black pepper, or to taste

Direction

- Preheat grill for medium heat and lightly oil the grate.
- Place ears onto the heated grill; roast corn until husks show burn marks on all sides and corn kernels are cooked through, about 20 minutes. Turn ears of corn often.

- Let corn ears cool until they can be handled; pull back husks and cut the roasted kernels from the ears. Place kernels into a large salad bowl.
- Lightly toss corn with black beans, plum tomatoes, green bell pepper, red onion, jalapeno peppers, lime juice, cilantro, and garlic. Pour tomato juice and tomato sauce over the salsa; toss again. Season with kosher salt and black pepper.
- Chill salsa at least 1 hour, preferably overnight.

Nutrition Information

- Calories: 129 calories
- Total Fat: 0.6 g
- Cholesterol: 0 mg
- Sodium: 363 mg
- Total Carbohydrate: 26.1 g
- Protein: 7.2 g

67. Salmon Tacos

"I am a newlywed and made these tacos after I had something similar at a restaurant in town. My husband loved them and thinks I am a brilliant chef and a perfect wife!"

Serving: 4 | Prep: 25 m | Cook: 25 m | Ready in: 50 m

Ingredients

- Salmon:
- 2 tablespoons butter
- 2 tablespoons lemon juice
- 1 dash Cajun seasoning
- 4 (3 ounce) fillets salmon fillets, thawed if frozen
- Salsa:
- 1 (15.25 ounce) can whole kernel corn, drained
- 1 (15 ounce) can black beans, drained
- 1 tomato, diced
- 1/4 cup diced red onion
- 1/4 cup chopped fresh cilantro
- 8 corn tortillas
- 1/2 cup shredded mild Cheddar cheese
- 1/2 cup sour cream (optional)
- 1/2 cup guacamole (optional)

Direction

- Preheat oven to 350 degrees F (175 degrees C).
- Microwave butter in a small microwave-safe bowl until melted, 20 to 30 seconds. Whisk in lemon juice. Add Cajun seasoning.

- Place salmon fillets in a shallow baking dish. Drizzle butter mixture over salmon.
- Bake salmon in the preheated oven until cooked through, about 20 minutes. Flake into smaller pieces with a fork.
- Mix corn, black beans, tomato, red onion, and cilantro in a bowl to make salsa.
- Arrange corn tortillas on a baking sheet.
- Warm tortillas in the preheated oven for about 5 minutes.
- Divide salmon, salsa, and Cheddar cheese among warm tortillas. Wrap up and serve with sour cream and guacamole.

Nutrition Information

- Calories: 650 calories
- Total Fat: 30.6 g
- Cholesterol: 84 mg
- Sodium: 980 mg
- Total Carbohydrate: 67.6 g
- Protein: 32.3 g

68. Sassy Spaghetti

"My husband is a spice hound and he loved this recipe."

Serving: 8 | Prep: 15 m | Cook: 15 m | Ready in: 30 m

Ingredients

- 1 (16 ounce) package spaghetti
- 1 tablespoon olive oil
- 1/2 onion, chopped
- 1 (15 ounce) can black beans, drained
- 1 (11 ounce) can sweet corn, drained
- 1 tablespoon ground cumin
- salt and pepper to taste
- 2 dashes hot sauce
- 3 tablespoons grated Parmesan cheese

Direction

- Bring a large pot of lightly salted water to a boil. Add pasta, cook for 8 to 10 minutes, until al dente, and drain.
- Heat the oil in a skillet over medium heat. Stir in the onion, beans, and corn. Season with cumin, salt, and pepper, and sprinkle with hot sauce. Cook and stir until onion is tender. Toss with cooked spaghetti and sprinkle with Parmesan cheese to serve.

Nutrition Information

- Calories: 251 calories

- Total Fat: 3.5 g
- Cholesterol: 2 mg
- Sodium: 151 mg
- Total Carbohydrate: 46.4 g
- Protein: 8.2 g

69. Six Can Chicken Tortilla Soup

"Delicious and EASY zesty soup recipe that uses only 6 canned ingredients! Serve over tortilla chips, and top with shredded Cheddar cheese. Throw away the cans and no one will know that it is not from scratch!"

Serving: 6 | Prep: 5 m | Cook: 15 m | Ready in: 20 m

Ingredients

- 1 (15 ounce) can whole kernel corn, drained
- 2 (14.5 ounce) cans chicken broth
- 1 (10 ounce) can chunk chicken
- 1 (15 ounce) can black beans
- 1 (10 ounce) can diced tomatoes with green chile peppers, drained

Direction

- Open the cans of corn, chicken broth, chunk chicken, black beans, and diced tomatoes with green chilies. Pour everything into a large saucepan or stock pot. Simmer over medium heat until chicken is heated through.

Nutrition Information

- Calories: 214 calories
- Total Fat: 4.9 g
- Cholesterol: 32 mg
- Sodium: 1482 mg
- Total Carbohydrate: 27.2 g
- Protein: 17.2 g

70. Slow Cooker Chicken Enchilada Soup

"Not quite a tortilla soup, not quite a taco soup, this comes together fast and gets better overnight. Stores like a dream and has fabulous flavor. Serve with sour cream and cheese on top, with either tortilla chips or cornbread on the side. Or if you're feeling fancy, you could make some paninis with pepper Jack cheese, roasted red peppers, avocados, tomatoes and mushrooms. Very tasty!"

Serving: 8 | Prep: 15 m | Cook: 6 h 15 m | Ready in: 6 h 30 m

Ingredients

- 4 cups chicken broth
- 2 (15 ounce) cans black beans, drained
- 2 (10 ounce) cans diced tomatoes with green chile peppers
- 1 (12 fluid ounce) can pale ale
- 1 (10 ounce) package frozen corn
- 1 (8 ounce) package red enchilada sauce (such as Frontera®)
- 1 onion, diced
- 1 (1.25 ounce) package taco seasoning
- 1 jalapeno pepper, seeded and diced
- 1 pound frozen chicken breasts
- 1 bunch cilantro, chopped

Direction

- Mix chicken broth, black beans, diced tomatoes, pale ale, corn, red enchilada sauce, onion, taco seasoning, and jalapeno pepper together in a slow cooker. Add whole chicken breasts.
- Cook on Low until an instant-read thermometer inserted into the center of the chicken reads at least 165 degrees F (74

degrees C), 5 to 6 hours. Remove chicken and shred using 2 forks; stir back into the slow cooker. Continue cooking, 1 to 2 hours more.
- Stir cilantro into the slow cooker. Cook on Low until flavors combine, about 15 minutes.

Nutrition Information

- Calories: 267 calories
- Total Fat: 2.7 g
- Cholesterol: 32 mg
- Sodium: 1595 mg
- Total Carbohydrate: 37.4 g
- Protein: 20.6 g

71. Slow Cooker Chicken Taco Bowls

"Make taco night easy night with these slow cooker chicken taco bowls! Made naturally gluten free with homemade low-sodium taco seasoning and layered with fresh vegetables, this low-calorie dinner is one everyone will love, especially the cook! Assemble bowls, add optional toppings, and devour!"

Serving: 6 | Prep: 20 m | Cook: 6 h 30 m | Ready in: 6 h 50 m

Ingredients

- Taco Seasoning:
- 1 tablespoon onion powder
- 1 teaspoon ground cumin
- 1 teaspoon dried oregano
- 1/2 teaspoon chili powder
- 1/2 teaspoon paprika
- 4 skinless, boneless chicken breasts
- 1 green bell pepper, cut into long slices
- 1 red bell pepper, cut into long slices
- salt and ground black pepper to taste
- 2 cups low-sodium chicken broth
- 2 (15 ounce) cans black beans, rinsed

Direction

- Combine onion powder, cumin, oregano, chili powder, and paprika together in a bowl to create taco seasoning.
- Place chicken breasts in the bottom of a slow cooker. Add green bell pepper, red bell pepper, salt, pepper, and taco

seasoning. Pour in broth, ensuring chicken is just covered in liquid.
- Set slow cooker to Low; cook for 6 hours.
- Break up chicken breasts with a wooden spoon. Add beans; cook on Low for 30 minutes more.

Nutrition Information

- Calories: 236 calories
- Total Fat: 2.6 g
- Cholesterol: 44 mg
- Sodium: 650 mg
- Total Carbohydrate: 27.3 g
- Protein: 26 g

72. Smokey Vegetarian Cuban Black Bean Soup

"This is a hearty and delicious soup even a meat-eater would love. Even better the second day. Substitute a poblano pepper for jalapeno pepper if desired."

Serving: 8 | Prep: 15 m | Cook: 1 h 25 m | Ready in: 9 h 40 m

Ingredients

- 1 pound dried black beans
- 1/4 cup vegetable oil
- 1 large yellow onion, finely chopped
- 1 tablespoon smoked paprika
- 2 teaspoons cumin seeds
- 1 red bell pepper, diced
- 1 green bell pepper, diced
- 8 cloves garlic, minced
- 2 teaspoons dried Mexican oregano, crushed between your fingers
- 2 bay leaves
- 6 cups vegetable stock
- 1 cup diced smoked tempeh bacon (such as Lightlife® Organic Smoky Tempeh Strips®)
- 2 tablespoons dark rum (optional)
- 1 jalapeño pepper, seeded and chopped
- 2 cups water
- 1 1/2 teaspoons salt
- salt and freshly ground black pepper to taste
- 1/2 cup sliced hard-boiled eggs (optional)
- 1/2 cup finely chopped red onion

Direction

- Place black beans into a large container and cover with several inches of cool water; let stand 8 hours to overnight. Drain beans and rinse with fresh water.
- Heat oil in a large Dutch oven or stockpot over medium heat; cook and stir yellow onion, paprika, and cumin seeds until fragrant, about 3 minutes. Add red bell pepper, green bell pepper, garlic, oregano, and bay leaves; cook and stir until onion is translucent and bell peppers are tender, 6 to 8 minutes.
- Mix vegetable stock, black beans, tempeh, rum, and jalapeno pepper into onion mixture. Increase heat to medium-high, bring to a simmer, reduce heat to medium-low, and cook until beans are tender, about 45 minutes.
- Pour water into bean mixture; season with 1 1/2 teaspoons salt. Cook, stirring occasionally, until beans begin to fall apart and soup thickens, 30 to 40 minutes; season with salt and pepper. Remove and discard bay leaves from soup.
- Ladle soup into bowls and garnish with hard-boiled eggs and red onion.

Nutrition Information

- Calories: 356 calories
- Total Fat: 10.2 g
- Cholesterol: 36 mg
- Sodium: 884 mg
- Total Carbohydrate: 47.5 g
- Protein: 18 g

73. Smoky Black Bean Burgers

"I had a hard time finding a black bean burger recipe that was not 'tex-mex,' so I made one up. Cook in a skillet or on the grill. Serve on buns with your favorite condiments."

Serving: 4 | Prep: 10 m | Cook: 10 m | Ready in: 55 m

Ingredients

- 1 tablespoon ground flax seed
- 3 tablespoons water
- 1 (15 ounce) can black beans - drained, rinsed, and mashed
- 1/4 cup panko bread crumbs
- 1 clove garlic, minced
- 1/2 teaspoon salt
- 1/2 tablespoon Worcestershire sauce
- 1/8 teaspoon liquid smoke flavoring
- cooking spray

Direction

- Mix ground flax seed and water together in a small bowl. Let sit to thicken, about 5 minutes.
- Mix flax mixture, black beans, panko bread crumbs, garlic, salt, Worcestershire sauce, and liquid smoke together in a bowl until combined. Form batter into 4 patties; arrange on a plate. Chill in refrigerator until set, about 30 minutes.
- Spray a skillet with cooking spray; place patties in skillet over medium heat. Cook until browned, about 5 minutes per side.

Nutrition Information

- Calories: 128 calories
- Total Fat: 1.5 g
- Cholesterol: 0 mg
- Sodium: 753 mg
- Total Carbohydrate: 23.4 g
- Protein: 7.5 g

74. Southwestern Egg Rolls with Avocado Cilantro Sauce

"Mix a blend of Southwestern-style ingredients to make a non-traditional egg roll that excites the palate from Chungah Rhee of Damn Delicious. The cilantro sauce takes the flavors to the next level."

Serving: 8 | Prep: 20 m | Cook: 20 m | Ready in: 40 m

Ingredients

- Cilantro Dipping Sauce:
- 3/4 cup loosely packed fresh cilantro leaves
- 1/3 cup sour cream
- 1 jalapeno pepper, seeded and deveined (optional)
- 2 tablespoons mayonnaise
- 1 clove garlic
- 1 lime, juiced
- Kosher salt and freshly ground pepper, to taste
- Egg Rolls:
- 2 avocados, halved, peeled, pitted
- 1 (15 ounce) can black beans, drained and rinsed
- 1 cup corn kernels (frozen, canned or roasted)
- 1 roma tomato, diced
- 1 lime, juiced
- 1 teaspoon chili powder
- 1/3 teaspoon ground cumin
- Kosher salt and freshly ground black pepper, to taste
- 8 egg roll wrappers
- Reynolds Wrap® Heavy Duty Aluminum Foil

Direction

- Preheat oven to 425 degrees F. Line a large baking pan with Reynolds Wrap(R) Heavy Duty Aluminum Foil. Grease or spray foil to prevent sticking.
- Combine cilantro, sour cream, jalapeno, mayonnaise, garlic and lime juice in the bowl of a food processor; season with salt and pepper to taste. Set aside.
- Mash avocados using a potato masher. Add black beans, corn, tomato, lime juice, chili powder, cumin and salt and pepper and gently toss to combine.
- Place avocado mixture in the center of each wrapper. Bring the bottom edge of the wrapper tightly over the filling, folding in the sides. Continue rolling until the top of the wrapper is reached. Using your finger, rub the edges of the wrapper with water, pressing to seal. Repeat with remaining wrappers and avocado mixture.
- Place egg rolls on the prepared baking dish. Lightly coat with nonstick spray.
- Place into oven and bake until golden brown and crisp, about 18 to 20 minutes.
- Serve immediately with cilantro dipping sauce.

Nutrition Information

- Calories: 225 calories
- Total Fat: 12.7 g
- Cholesterol: 6 mg
- Sodium: 385 mg
- Total Carbohydrate: 25.2 g
- Protein: 6.3 g

75. Spicy Black and Red Bean Soup

"Simple to prepare! Throw it in your crock pot in the morning, and it will be done when you get home from work! I use fat-free, low-sodium chicken broth, and no-salt-added diced tomatoes."

Serving: 10 | Prep: 15 m | Cook: 1 h 10 m | Ready in: 1 h 25 m

Ingredients

- 1 tablespoon vegetable oil
- 1 1/2 cups chopped onion
- 1 1/4 cups sliced carrots
- 2 cloves garlic, minced
- 3 cups chicken broth
- 2 teaspoons white sugar
- 1 (16 ounce) package frozen shoepeg corn
- 1 (15 ounce) can kidney beans, drained and rinsed
- 1 (15 ounce) can black beans, rinsed and drained
- 1 (14.5 ounce) can Italian-style stewed tomatoes
- 1 (14.5 ounce) can diced tomatoes, drained
- 1 (4 ounce) can diced green chiles

Direction

- Heat the oil in a large Dutch oven over medium-high heat until hot. Add onion, carrot, and garlic; sauté 5 minutes. Stir in broth, sugar, corn, beans, tomatoes, and chilies; bring to a boil. Cover, reduce heat, and simmer 2 hours.
- This soup can also be prepared in a crock pot. Combine everything in the pot, and cook on HIGH for the first hour. Turn

the temperature down to LOW, and cook 7 more hours.

Nutrition Information

- Calories: 172 calories
- Total Fat: 2.5 g
- Cholesterol: 0 mg
- Sodium: 775 mg
- Total Carbohydrate: 29.9 g
- Protein: 8.4 g

76. Spicy Three Bean Soup

"This wonderfully hearty soup is great for chilly fall or winter nights. Three types of beans and plenty of vegetables combine in this flavorful medley. Dry beans may be substituted, but will require soaking overnight."

Serving: 12 | Prep: 20 m | Cook: 25 m | Ready in: 45 m

Ingredients

- 1/4 cup olive oil
- 1 onion, diced
- 2 cloves garlic, diced
- 2 (16 ounce) cans great Northern beans, rinsed and drained
- 2 (15.25 ounce) cans red kidney beans, rinsed and drained
- 1 (15 ounce) can black beans, rinsed and drained
- 3 stalks celery, chopped
- 3 carrots, chopped
- 2 large potatoes, cubed
- 15 ounces tomato-vegetable juice cocktail
- 2 tablespoons brown sugar
- 1 1/2 teaspoons dried thyme
- 4 cups water
- 2 cubes vegetable bouillon
- 1 cup red wine

Direction

- Heat the olive oil in a large saucepan over medium heat. Place onion and garlic in the saucepan and slowly cook and stir until tender and browned.

- Place the great northern beans, red kidney beans, black beans, celery, carrots, potatoes, tomato-vegetable juice cocktail, brown sugar, thyme, water and vegetable bouillon in the saucepan. Cook over medium-high heat approximately 25 minutes. As the mixture thickens, stir in the red wine.

Nutrition Information

- Calories: 310 calories
- Total Fat: 5.5 g
- Cholesterol: 2 mg
- Sodium: 393 mg
- Total Carbohydrate: 51 g
- Protein: 11.3 g

77. Spinach and Black Bean Pasta

"This is a very tasty and easy vegetarian pasta dish. It takes minimal time to prepare and has amazing flavor! It's also great served with brown rice!"

Serving: 8 | Prep: 15 m | Cook: 30 m | Ready in: 45 m

Ingredients

- 1 (16 ounce) package whole wheat rotini pasta
- 1 1/2 cups vegetable broth
- 2 1/2 cups chopped fresh spinach
- 1/2 cup chopped red onion
- 1 clove garlic, chopped
- 1/2 teaspoon cayenne pepper
- salt and pepper to taste
- 1 (15 ounce) can black beans, drained and rinsed
- 1 cup frozen chopped broccoli
- 1 cup diced tomatoes
- 2 ounces freshly grated Parmesan cheese

Direction

- Bring a large pot of lightly salted water to a boil. Add rotini, and cook for 8 to 10 minutes, or until al dente; drain.
- In a large saucepan over medium heat, bring the vegetable broth to a boil. Reduce heat, and mix in spinach, onion, garlic, cayenne pepper, salt, and pepper. Stir in the black beans and broccoli. Continue to cook and stir 5 to 10 minutes.
- Stir the tomatoes into the saucepan, and continue cooking 10 minutes, or until all vegetables are tender. Serve over the cooked pasta. Garnish with Parmesan cheese.

Nutrition Information

- Calories: 279 calories
- Total Fat: 3.2 g
- Cholesterol: 6 mg
- Sodium: 463 mg
- Total Carbohydrate: 51.1 g
- Protein: 14.9 g

78. Stacked Fajita Vegetable Enchilada Casserole

"This has become a staple meal at our house. It is a great way to help use refrigerator delights (leftovers) or to make from scratch. It is a tasty dish we have served to our meat-eating friends and family with rave reviews. The 'cheese' sauce could be substituted for real cheese. Use your choice of red, yellow, green, or orange bell peppers, and black beans, kidney beans, or pinto beans."

Serving: 8 | Prep: 30 m | Cook: 45 m | Ready in: 1 h 25 m

Ingredients

- 1/2 zucchini, cut into 1/4-inch slices
- 1 cup red bell pepper slices
- 1 onion, cut into 1/4-inch slices and separated into rings
- 1 cup water
- 1 teaspoon vegetable oil
- 1 (1.27 ounce) packet dry fajita seasoning
- 1/2 cup all-purpose flour
- 1/2 cup nutritional yeast
- 1 teaspoon salt
- 1 1/2 teaspoons garlic powder
- 1/2 teaspoon dry mustard powder
- 2 cups water
- 1/4 cup margarine
- 2 (10 ounce) cans red enchilada sauce
- 5 (9 inch) whole-wheat tortillas, torn into 1-inch pieces
- 1 1/2 cups cooked brown rice
- 3 (15 ounce) cans black beans, rinsed and drained
- 1 tablespoon sliced black olives (optional)
- 1/4 avocado - peeled, pitted and diced (optional)

- 2 tablespoons chopped tomato (optional)
- 1 jalapeno pepper, seeded and thinly sliced (optional)
- 2 tablespoons chopped onion (optional)
- 2 tablespoons prepared salsa (optional)
- 2 tablespoons sour cream (optional)

Direction

- Preheat oven to 350 degrees F (175 degrees C).
- Place zucchini, red bell pepper, and 1 onion sliced into rings into a bowl; stir in 1 cup water, vegetable oil, and dry fajita seasoning. (Mixture can be left to marinate 1 to 2 hours, if desired.) Drain vegetables.
- Heat vegetables in a large skillet over medium heat. Cook and stir until soft and slightly browned, about 10 minutes; transfer to a bowl and set aside.
- Place flour, nutritional yeast, salt, garlic powder, and dry mustard powder into a saucepan and whisk in 2 cups water until thoroughly combined.
- Place saucepan over medium heat and bring the mixture to a boil; reduce heat to low and simmer, whisking constantly until thick, about 5 minutes.
- Stir in margarine and remove sauce from heat.
- Pour 1/2 can of enchilada sauce into bottom of a 9x13-inch baking dish and spread the sauce out to cover the bottom. Top with 1/4 of the tortilla pieces, and spread 1/2 cup brown rice onto the tortillas.
- Spread 1/3 of the cooked vegetables over the brown rice.
- Spread 1 can of black beans over the vegetables; cover beans with 1/4 of the nutritional yeast sauce.
- Repeat the layers twice more.
- Make a final layer containing remaining 1/4 of the tortilla pieces, remaining nutritional yeast sauce, and remaining 1/2

can enchilada sauce.
- Bake casserole in the preheated oven until bubbling, 30 to 45 minutes; allow to stand for 10 minutes.
- Top casserole with optional black olives, avocado, tomato, jalapeno pepper, 2 tablespoons of chopped onion, salsa, and sour cream before serving.

Nutrition Information

- Calories: 457 calories
- Total Fat: 11.2 g
- Cholesterol: 2 mg
- Sodium: 1678 mg
- Total Carbohydrate: 77.4 g
- Protein: 20.5 g

79. Steel Mill Chili

"This is a quick, easy, and delicious chili recipe from my father-in-law who works in the steel mills of Northwest Indiana. Best if served with sour cream and grated Cheddar cheese. Enjoy!"

Serving: 6 | Prep: 10 m | Cook: 40 m | Ready in: 50 m

Ingredients

- 1 pound ground beef
- 1 onion, chopped
- 1 (15 ounce) can black beans
- 1 (14.5 ounce) can diced tomatoes
- 1 (15.25 ounce) can sweet corn
- 1 (1.25 ounce) package chili seasoning mix
- 1/8 teaspoon ground cumin, or to taste
- 1/8 teaspoon chili powder, or to taste
- 1 pinch salt to taste (optional)

Direction

- Heat a large skillet over medium-high heat. Cook and stir beef and onion in the hot skillet until browned and crumbly, 5 to 7 minutes; drain and discard grease.
- Mix black beans, diced tomatoes, and sweet corn into beef mixture; add chili seasoning mix, cumin, chili powder, and salt and mix well. Bring liquid to a boil; reduce heat and simmer until chili is cooked through and flavors have combined, about 30 minutes.

Nutrition Information

- Calories: 315 calories
- Total Fat: 12.8 g
- Cholesterol: 46 mg
- Sodium: 1215 mg
- Total Carbohydrate: 31 g
- Protein: 19.9 g

80. Stuffed Green Peppers

"When I was little, my family often ate meat-stuffed peppers. This veggie alternative came from my imagination."

Serving: 4 | Prep: 15 m | Cook: 1 h 5 m | Ready in: 1 h 20 m

Ingredients

- 1 cup uncooked white rice
- 1 (15 ounce) can black beans, drained and rinsed
- 1 tablespoon chili powder
- 4 green bell peppers
- 16 slices Swiss cheese
- 1 (15 ounce) can tomato sauce

Direction

- Preheat oven to 400 degrees F (200 degrees C).
- In a saucepan bring 2 cups water to a boil. Add rice and stir. Reduce heat, cover and simmer for 20 minutes.
- Combine cooked rice with black beans and chili powder. Cut the tops off of the peppers and remove the ribs and seeds. Spoon about 2 tablespoons of the rice and bean mixture into the bottoms of the peppers. Lay a slice of cheese on top and repeat 3 more times, ending with cheese on top.
- Bake in preheated oven until peppers soften, about 45 minutes.
- Meanwhile, heat tomato sauce in a small saucepan over low to medium heat. Slice peppers in half, top with tomato sauce and serve.

Nutrition Information

- Calories: 675 calories
- Total Fat: 32.7 g
- Cholesterol: 104 mg
- Sodium: 792 mg
- Total Carbohydrate: 59.6 g
- Protein: 37 g

81. Summer Salad with CuminCrusted Salmon

"For the greatest omega-3 benefit buy the fattiest fish. Try mackerel, anchovies, herring, sardines, salmon, tuna and turbot. Frozen and canned are OK, the USDA says."

Serving: 4

Ingredients

- Salad:
- 2 ounces pine nuts
- 5 cups mixed greens
- 1 (15 ounce) can black beans, drained and rinsed
- 1 cup scallions, sliced
- 1 large orange, cut in 1-inch chunks
- 1/2 cup feta cheese, crumbled
- 1 cup cilantro, chopped
- Dressing:
- 2 tablespoons orange juice concentrate
- 4 tablespoons olive oil
- 1/2 teaspoon cumin
- 1 1/2 tablespoons balsamic vinegar
- 2 garlic cloves, crushed
- 1/4 teaspoon salt
- Cumin-Crusted Salmon:
- 1 1/2 tablespoons cumin
- 2 teaspoons paprika
- 1/4 teaspoon salt
- 1/4 teaspoon freshly ground black pepper
- 1 pound salmon fillet, skin removed

Direction

- Heat a non-stick skillet, add pine nuts and stir until toasty, about 5 minutes. In a large bowl, place all salad ingredients (reserve half of the cilantro and half of the pine nuts for garnish).
- In a separate bowl, stir dressing ingredients together.
- In a bowl, combine cumin, paprika, salt and pepper. Cut salmon in 8 strips and coat with spices. Grill (or sear in a non-stick skillet brushed with canola oil) until crusty.
- Toss salad and dressing; divide on plates. Top with salmon and reserved cilantro and pine nuts.

Nutrition Information

- Calories: 639 calories
- Total Fat: 39.7 g
- Cholesterol: 84 mg
- Sodium: 1139 mg
- Total Carbohydrate: 37.3 g
- Protein: 37.1 g

82. Superfood Hummus

"This is a hummus which your body would love!"

Serving: 16 | Prep: 15 m | Ready in: 15 m

Ingredients

- 1 cup drained canned (low sodium) garbanzo beans, half of the liquid reserved
- 1 cup drained canned (low sodium) black beans, half of the liquid reserved
- 1/2 cup tahini
- 1/4 cup extra-virgin olive oil
- 1 lemon, juiced
- 2 tablespoons chia seeds
- 2 tablespoons flax seeds
- 1 tablespoon ground cumin
- 2 cloves garlic, minced
- salt to taste
- 1 pinch paprika, or to taste
- 1 tablespoon chopped fresh cilantro, or to taste
- 1 tablespoon chopped roasted red bell peppers, or to taste

Direction

- Place garbanzo beans and 1/2 their juice, black beans and 1/2 their juice, tahini, olive oil, lemon juice, chia seeds, flax seeds, cumin, garlic, salt, and paprika in a blender; process until a smooth hummus forms. Transfer hummus to a serving bowl and garnish with cilantro and roasted red peppers.

Nutrition Information

- Calories: 117 calories
- Total Fat: 8.7 g
- Cholesterol: 0 mg
- Sodium: 24 mg
- Total Carbohydrate: 7.1 g
- Protein: 3.4 g

83. Taco Mix with Black Beans

"My kids gobble this filling up, and it has the benefit of being easy to make and nutritious, too! Serve with taco shells and top with lettuce and cheese. My favorite use is on a taco salad with cheese, tortilla strips, salsa, ranch dressing, romaine lettuce, and peppers. Yummy!"

Serving: 8 | Prep: 5 m | Cook: 10 m | Ready in: 15 m

Ingredients

- 1 pound lean ground beef
- 1 (19 ounce) can black beans, rinsed and drained
- 1/2 cup salsa
- 1/4 cup water
- 2 tablespoons taco seasoning mix

Direction

- Heat a large skillet over medium heat. Cook and stir beef in the hot skillet until browned and crumbly, 5 to 7 minutes.
- Stir black beans with the ground beef; add salsa, water, and taco seasoning mix. Cook, stirring frequently, until the mixture is heated through, 5 to 7 minutes.

Nutrition Information

- Calories: 182 calories
- Total Fat: 7.1 g
- Cholesterol: 37 mg
- Sodium: 554 mg
- Total Carbohydrate: 13.7 g

- Protein: 15.1 g

84. Tex Mex Black Bean Dip

"This black bean dip is great served with corn or flour tortilla chips. Serve warm or at room temperature."

Serving: 16 | Prep: 10 m | Cook: 10 m | Ready in: 20 m

Ingredients

- 1 (15 ounce) can black beans, rinsed and drained
- 1 teaspoon vegetable oil
- 1/2 cup chopped onion
- 2 cloves garlic, minced
- 1/2 cup fresh corn kernels
- 3/4 cup chopped tomatoes
- 1/2 cup mild picante sauce
- 1 teaspoon ground cumin
- 1 teaspoon chili powder
- 1/2 cup shredded Monterey Jack cheese
- 1/4 cup chopped fresh cilantro
- 1 tablespoon fresh lime juice

Direction

- Place black beans in a medium size mixing bowl, partially mash beans -- beans should remain a little chunky.
- In a medium size frying pan, heat oil over a medium heat. Stir in onion and garlic and sauté for 4 minutes.
- Mix beans, corn, tomato, picante sauce, cumin, and chili powder into the frying pan; cook for 5 minutes or until thickened. Remove the pan from the heat, mix in cheese, cilantro and lime juice; stir until cheese is melted.

Nutrition Information

- Calories: 50 calories
- Total Fat: 1.7 g
- Cholesterol: 3 mg
- Sodium: 149 mg
- Total Carbohydrate: 5.9 g
- Protein: 2.7 g

85. TexMex Turkey Chili with Black Beans Corn and Butternut Squash

"Easy to make and ready in just 30 minutes. Butternut squash adds a twist of sweetness to this chili."

Serving: 6 | Prep: 10 m | Cook: 20 m | Ready in: 30 m

Ingredients

- 1/4 cup Mazola® Corn Oil
- 1 pound ground turkey
- 1 cup diced onion
- 1 teaspoon minced garlic
- 2 tablespoons chili powder
- 1 tablespoon ground cumin
- 1 tablespoon chicken-flavored bouillon powder or tomato-flavored bouillon
- 1 (15 ounce) can black beans, rinsed and drained
- 1 (11 ounce) can Mexi-corn, drained
- 1 (12 ounce) package frozen diced butternut squash, thawed
- 1 (28 ounce) can crushed tomatoes or tomato sauce
- 1 cup water
- 1/3 cup ketchup
- Garnishes:
- Shredded Mexican cheese, fresh cilantro, lime wedges, avocado slice

Direction

- Heat oil in large 4 to 6-quart saucepan over medium heat and add turkey. Brown turkey for 5 to 7 minutes, breaking apart.
- Add onions, garlic, chili powder, cumin and bouillon powder and cook for 3 to 5 minutes or until onions soften. Stir in vegetables, tomatoes, water and ketchup. Bring to a boil; reduce heat to low and simmer for 10 minutes. To serve, ladle into bowls and top with desired garnishes.
- Recipe note: If using fresh butternut squash, microwave for 1 to 2 minutes before adding to the chili or allow extra cooking time to ensure tenderness.

Nutrition Information

- Calories: 411 calories
- Total Fat: 17.2 g
- Cholesterol: 57 mg
- Sodium: 1039 mg
- Total Carbohydrate: 46.8 g
- Protein: 25.1 g

86. The Best Turkey Chili

"This is just the best tasting chili. My family prefers it over beef chili. I like to put out toppings such as chopped onion, cilantro, chopped bell pepper, cheese, and sour cream and let everyone serve themselves."

Serving: 14 | Prep: 15 m | Cook: 2 h 15 m | Ready in: 2 h 30 m

Ingredients

- 2 pounds ground turkey
- 1 (28 ounce) can crushed tomatoes
- 1 (15 ounce) can tomato sauce
- 1 (15.5 ounce) can kidney beans, rinsed and drained
- 1 (15.5 ounce) can pinto beans, rinsed and drained
- 1 (15.5 ounce) can black beans, rinsed and drained
- 1/2 cup chopped onion
- 1 clove garlic, minced
- 1/4 cup red wine
- 2 tablespoons chili powder
- 1 teaspoon ground cumin
- 1 teaspoon dried parsley
- 1 teaspoon dried oregano
- 1/2 teaspoon black pepper
- 1/4 teaspoon crushed red pepper flakes (optional)
- 2 bay leaves

Direction

- Cook and stir the ground turkey in a large pot over medium heat until crumbly and no longer pink, about 5 minutes. Stir in the crushed tomatoes, tomato sauce, kidney beans, pinto beans, black beans, onion, garlic, and red wine. Season with chili powder, cumin, parsley, oregano, black pepper, red pepper flakes, and bay leaves. Bring to a simmer over medium-high heat, then reduce heat to medium-low, cover, and simmer 2 hours. Stir the chili occasionally as it simmers. Remove and discard bay leaves before serving.

Nutrition Information

- Calories: 214 calories
- Total Fat: 5.8 g
- Cholesterol: 48 mg
- Sodium: 562 mg
- Total Carbohydrate: 22.2 g
- Protein: 19.6 g

87. ThreeBean Vegetarian Chili

"Hearty, meatless chili with plenty of veggies."

Serving: 6 | Prep: 30 m | Cook: 45 m | Ready in: 1 h 15 m

Ingredients

- 1/4 cup vegetable oil
- 1 onion, cut into small dice
- 1 red bell pepper, cut into small dice
- 1 green bell pepper, cut into small dice
- 1 jalapeno pepper, seeded and minced
- 4 cloves garlic, minced
- 1/8 teaspoon salt
- 2 tablespoons chili powder
- 2 teaspoons ground cumin
- 2 teaspoons dried oregano
- 1/2 (6 ounce) can tomato paste
- 1 (28 ounce) can diced tomatoes
- 1 3/4 cups water
- 1 (15.5 ounce) can black beans
- 1 (15.5 ounce) can kidney beans
- 1 (15.5 ounce) can chickpeas
- Sour cream, shredded Cheddar cheese, fresh cilantro leaves (optional)

Direction

- Heat oil in a heavy 6-quart pot over medium heat. Cook onion, bell peppers, jalapeno, garlic, and salt, stirring occasionally, until tender, about 10 minutes. Stir in chili powder, cumin,

oregano, tomato paste, tomatoes, and water and simmer over medium-low heat, stirring occasionally, until thickened, about 20 minutes.
- Drain beans, reserving liquid, and rinse under cold water. Add beans and 3/4 cup reserved liquid to chili and simmer, stirring occasionally, until heated through, 5 to 7 minutes.
- Top each serving with sour cream, cheese, and cilantro (if using).

Nutrition Information

- Calories: 377 calories
- Total Fat: 11.3 g
- Cholesterol: 0 mg
- Sodium: 1060 mg
- Total Carbohydrate: 55.7 g
- Protein: 15.2 g

88. Val and Jesss Vegan Avocado Dip

"We love avocados, and invented this dip together. It is super easy, and you can adjust the amounts of ingredients to suit your taste. It has been a party favorite ever since, and the majority of requests are from the meat lovers! Serve with blue corn chips."

Serving: 12 | Prep: 15 m | Ready in: 15 m

Ingredients

- 2 avocados - peeled, pitted and diced
- 1 (19 ounce) can black beans, drained and rinsed
- 1 (11 ounce) can whole kernel corn, drained
- 1 medium onion, minced
- 3/4 cup salsa
- 1 tablespoon chopped fresh cilantro
- 1 tablespoon lemon juice
- 2 tablespoons chili powder
- salt and pepper to taste

Direction

- In a bowl, mix the avocados, black beans, corn, onion, salsa, cilantro, and lemon juice. Season with chili powder, salt, and pepper.

Nutrition Information

- Calories: 128 calories

- Total Fat: 5.5 g
- Cholesterol: 0 mg
- Sodium: 362 mg
- Total Carbohydrate: 17.8 g
- Protein: 4.6 g

89. Vegan Black Bean and Sweet Potato Salad

"This is a great side dish using fresh ingredients. There are never leftovers!"

Serving: 4 | Prep: 15 m | Cook: 25 m | Ready in: 40 m

Ingredients

- 1 pound sweet potatoes, peeled and cut into 3/4-inch cubes
- 3 tablespoons olive oil, divided
- 1/2 teaspoon ground cumin, or more to taste
- 1/4 teaspoon red pepper flakes (optional)
- coarse salt and ground black pepper to taste
- 2 tablespoons freshly squeezed lime juice
- 1 (14.5 ounce) can black beans, rinsed and drained
- 1/2 red onion, finely chopped
- 1/2 cup chopped fresh cilantro

Direction

- Preheat oven to 450 degrees F (230 degrees C).
- Spread sweet potatoes onto a rimmed baking sheet. Drizzle 1 tablespoon olive oil over sweet potatoes; season with cumin, red pepper flakes, salt, and pepper. Toss sweet potatoes until evenly coated.
- Roast on the lower rack of the preheated oven, stirring halfway through, until sweet potatoes are tender, 25 to 35 minutes.
- Whisk remaining 2 tablespoons olive oil and lime juice together in a large bowl; season with salt and pepper. Add sweet potatoes, black beans, onion, and cilantro; gently toss to coat.

Nutrition Information

- Calories: 291 calories
- Total Fat: 10.6 g
- Cholesterol: 0 mg
- Sodium: 462 mg
- Total Carbohydrate: 42.2 g
- Protein: 8.4 g

90. Vegan Fajitas

"This is a wonderful meatless version of traditional fajitas! It can be prepared in advance, or right away."

Serving: 6 | Prep: 20 m | Cook: 20 m | Ready in: 1 h 10 m

Ingredients

- 1/4 cup olive oil
- 1/4 cup red wine vinegar
- 1 teaspoon dried oregano
- 1 teaspoon chili powder
- garlic salt to taste
- salt and pepper to taste
- 1 teaspoon white sugar
- 2 small zucchini, julienned
- 2 medium small yellow squash, julienned
- 1 large onion, sliced
- 1 green bell pepper, cut into thin strips
- 1 red bell pepper, cut into thin strips
- 2 tablespoons olive oil
- 1 (8.75 ounce) can whole kernel corn, drained
- 1 (15 ounce) can black beans, drained

Direction

- In a large bowl combine olive oil, vinegar, oregano, chili powder, garlic salt, salt, pepper and sugar. To the marinade add the zucchini, yellow squash, onion, green pepper and red pepper. Marinate vegetables in the refrigerator for at least 30 minutes, but not more than 24 hours.

- Heat oil in a large skillet over medium-high heat. Drain the vegetables and sauté until tender, about 10 to 15 minutes. Stir in the corn and beans; increase the heat to high for 5 minutes, to brown vegetables.

Nutrition Information

- Calories: 198 calories
- Total Fat: 14.4 g
- Cholesterol: 0 mg
- Sodium: 130 mg
- Total Carbohydrate: 17.9 g
- Protein: 3 g

91. Vegan Sweet Potato Enchiladas

"This vegan enchiladas dish is one of our favorites and finds its way onto our dinner table every week. Try serving them with guacamole on top along with rice."

Serving: 8 | Prep: 20 m | Cook: 44 m | Ready in: 1 h 4 m

Ingredients

- 1 large sweet potato, chopped
- 2 tablespoons olive oil
- 1 onion, chopped
- 3 cloves garlic, minced, or more to taste
- 2 (15.5 ounce) cans black beans, drained and rinsed
- 1 green bell pepper, chopped
- 1 (16 ounce) bag frozen chopped spinach, thawed and drained
- 1 tablespoon lime juice, or to taste
- 1 teaspoon ground cumin, or more to taste
- 1 teaspoon cayenne pepper
- salt to taste
- 3 cups enchilada sauce, divided
- 8 (8 inch) flour tortillas

Direction

- Preheat the oven to 350 degrees F (175 degrees C).
- Place a steamer insert into a saucepan and fill with water to just below the bottom of the steamer. Bring water to a boil. Add sweet potato, cover, and steam until tender, 2 to 6 minutes.

- Heat olive oil in a skillet over medium heat. Add onion; cook and stir until translucent, about 5 minutes. Add garlic; cook and stir until fragrant, 2 to 4 minutes. Add the steamed sweet potato, black beans, green bell pepper, spinach, lime juice, cumin, cayenne pepper, and salt. Cook until flavors blend, about 5 minutes. Add 2 cups enchilada sauce; cook until slightly absorbed, about 5 minutes more.
- Spoon 1 to 2 cups enchilada mixture into the bottom of a 9x13-inch baking dish and about 1 cup into each tortilla. Arrange filled tortillas in the baking dish. Pour remaining 1 cup enchilada sauce over the tortillas.
- Bake in the preheated oven until sauce is deep red and enchiladas are heated through, about 20 minutes.

Nutrition Information

- Calories: 407 calories
- Total Fat: 9.6 g
- Cholesterol: 0 mg
- Sodium: 999 mg
- Total Carbohydrate: 67.2 g
- Protein: 14 g

92. Vegan Yuca Tacos

"A vegan way to enjoy tacos in the summertime. A twist on soft tacos without losing the classic flavor."

Serving: 10 | Prep: 15 m | Cook: 40 m | Ready in: 55 m

Ingredients

- 1 1/2 pounds frozen yuca
- 1 cup frozen corn
- 1 medium green bell pepper, diced
- 1 medium onion, diced
- salt to taste
- 1 (16 ounce) can black beans, rinsed and drained
- 3 tablespoons olive oil, divided, or as needed
- 10 (6 inch) corn tortillas
- 10 toothpicks

Direction

- Place yuca into a large pot and cover with salted water; bring to a boil. Reduce heat to medium-low and simmer until tender, 20 to 25 minutes. Drain.
- Preheat an outdoor grill for medium heat and lightly oil the grate.
- Combine corn, bell pepper, and onion in an aluminum pan. Add 1 tablespoon olive oil, or enough to coat the vegetables and the bottom of the pan. Cook on the grill, stirring every 5 minutes, until pepper is tender and onion is translucent, 10 to 20 minutes. Remove from heat.

- Mash yuca and black beans together in a large bowl until smooth and well blended, adding about 1 tablespoon olive oil as needed. Add the grilled vegetables; mix well, kneading by hand if necessary.
- Warm tortillas in the microwave, 30 seconds to 1 minute. Add equal amounts of the yuca mixture to the tortillas. Fold each taco in half over the filling and secure with a toothpick. Paint the top of each tortilla with remaining olive oil.
- Place the tacos on a grill topper. Grill for about 5 minutes. Remove from heat and remove the toothpicks.

Nutrition Information

- Calories: 235 calories
- Total Fat: 5.1 g
- Cholesterol: 0 mg
- Sodium: 207 mg
- Total Carbohydrate: 42.6 g
- Protein: 7.3 g

93. Vegetarian Black Bean Burritos

"This is one of our favorite summer dinners - a black bean vegetarian burrito. Full of flavor and good for you too! Serve on flour or corn tortillas with cheese, sour cream or yogurt, tomatoes, and whatever burrito toppings you like!"

Serving: 4 | Prep: 20 m | Cook: 10 m | Ready in: 30 m

Ingredients

- 2 tablespoons olive oil
- 1 tablespoon white vinegar
- 5 dashes hot sauce
- 1/2 teaspoon salt
- 1/8 teaspoon ground black pepper
- 2 cloves garlic, minced, or more to taste
- 1/4 onion, chopped
- 1 onion, thinly sliced
- 1/2 small zucchini, cut into small chunks
- 1/4 (6 ounce) can sliced black olives
- 1 cup shredded Cabbage
- 1 tablespoon sliced jalapeno pepper, or to taste
- 1 (15 ounce) can black beans, rinsed and drained
- 4 burrito-size tortillas, or as needed

Direction

- Whisk olive oil, vinegar, hot sauce, salt, and black pepper together in a microwave-safe glass or ceramic bowl.
- Layer garlic, chopped onion, sliced onion, zucchini, olives, cabbage, jalapeno, and black beans, respectively, over hot

sauce mixture. Cover the bowl with plastic wrap and poke a few holes in the top.
- Microwave for 5 minutes; stir, recover with plastic wrap, and microwave until filling is hot throughout, about 5 minutes more.
- Spoon hot filling in a line across the middle of a tortilla. Fold opposing edges of the tortilla to overlap the filling. Roll 1 of the opposing edges around the filling into a burrito. Repeat with remaining tortillas and filling.

Nutrition Information

- Calories: 417 calories
- Total Fat: 13.9 g
- Cholesterol: 0 mg
- Sodium: 1289 mg
- Total Carbohydrate: 60.6 g
- Protein: 13.4 g

94. Veggie Pizzadillas

"I make this for Meatless (lacto-ovo) Monday Meals. It is a big hit! The flavor profile is complex and savory and you can add a dash of hot sauce to spice things up even more. I cut the pizzadillas in half for the kids."

Serving: 4 | Prep: 15 m | Cook: 25 m | Ready in: 40 m

Ingredients

- 4 (6 inch) flour tortillas
- 2 tablespoons olive oil, divided, or as needed
- 1 onion, thinly sliced
- 1 poblano chile, diced
- 1 red bell pepper, diced
- 2 cloves garlic, minced
- 1 (15 ounce) can black beans, rinsed and drained
- 1 cup frozen corn, thawed
- 1/4 teaspoon dried oregano
- salt to taste
- 1/4 cup mild enchilada sauce
- 1 cup shredded Mexican cheese blend
- 1/4 cup sour cream
- 1/2 cup crumbled queso fresco
- 1/4 cup chopped fresh cilantro
- 1 dash hot pepper sauce (optional)

Direction

- Preheat oven to 400 degrees F (200 degrees C). Place tortillas on baking sheet covered with foil; lightly brush each with olive oil, and prick all over with fork.

- Bake tortillas in the preheated oven until they are puffed and golden, 5 to 6 minutes. Remove from oven and allow to cool on cooling rack.
- Heat remaining olive oil in a large skillet over medium heat. Add onion, poblano chile, and red bell pepper; cook and stir until onions are translucent and lightly browned, 8 to 10 minutes. Stir in black beans, corn, garlic, oregano, and salt; cook and stir until mixture is heated through, about 5 minutes.
- Return tortillas to the foil-lined baking sheet in a single layer; spoon 1 tablespoon enchilada sauce over each tortilla. Top with 1/4 of the black bean and corn mixture and 1/4 of the shredded Mexican cheese.
- Bake pizzadillas in the preheated oven until cheese has melted, 5 to 6 minutes.
- Remove pizzadillas from oven; top each with sour cream, queso fresco, and cilantro. Add a dash of hot pepper sauce to each slice.

Nutrition Information

- Calories: 547 calories
- Total Fat: 26.8 g
- Cholesterol: 49 mg
- Sodium: 1014 mg
- Total Carbohydrate: 56.1 g
- Protein: 23.7 g

95. Zesty Quinoa Salad

"This bright and colorful salad is a great summertime recipe (or anytime you want to feel like it's summertime). Light and citrusy, it's a whole new way to enjoy quinoa. Lime juice and cilantro give a refreshing kick, while quinoa and black beans provide tasty vegan protein. If you're not vegan, add even more protein by adding chunks of chicken or turkey. Yum!"

Serving: 6 | Prep: 20 m | Cook: 10 m | Ready in: 30 m

Ingredients

- 1 cup quinoa
- 2 cups water
- 1/4 cup extra-virgin olive oil
- 2 limes, juiced
- 2 teaspoons ground cumin
- 1 teaspoon salt
- 1/2 teaspoon red pepper flakes, or more to taste
- 1 1/2 cups halved cherry tomatoes
- 1 (15 ounce) can black beans, drained and rinsed
- 5 green onions, finely chopped
- 1/4 cup chopped fresh cilantro
- salt and ground black pepper to taste

Direction

- Bring quinoa and water to a boil in a saucepan. Reduce heat to medium-low, cover, and simmer until quinoa is tender and water has been absorbed, 10 to 15 minutes. Set aside to cool.
- Whisk olive oil, lime juice, cumin, 1 teaspoon salt, and red pepper flakes together in a bowl.

- Combine quinoa, tomatoes, black beans, and green onions together in a bowl. Pour dressing over quinoa mixture; toss to coat. Stir in cilantro; season with salt and black pepper. Serve immediately or chill in refrigerator.

Nutrition Information

- Calories: 270 calories
- Total Fat: 11.5 g
- Cholesterol: 0 mg
- Sodium: 675 mg
- Total Carbohydrate: 33.8 g
- Protein: 8.9 g

Chapter 2: Black-Eyed Beans
***

96. Avocado and Black Eyed Pea Salsa

"A rich and flavorful chip dip!"

Serving: 12 | Prep: 20 m | Ready in: 1 h 20 m

Ingredients

- 2 ripe but firm avocados, diced
- 1/2 cup chopped green onion
- 1/2 cup chopped fresh cilantro
- 1 cup chopped roma (plum) tomatoes
- 1 (11 ounce) can shoepeg corn, drained
- 1 (15 ounce) can black-eyed peas, rinsed and drained
- 1/4 cup red wine vinegar
- 1/4 cup olive oil
- 1 teaspoon ground cumin
- 1/2 teaspoon minced garlic
- salt and black pepper to taste

Direction

- Lightly mix together avocados, green onion, cilantro, tomatoes, corn, and black-eyed peas in a salad bowl until well combined.
- Whisk together red wine vinegar, olive oil, cumin, and minced garlic in a bowl, and pour over the salad. Season to taste with salt and pepper, and lightly toss the salad again. Chill for 1 hour before serving, to blend the flavors.

Nutrition Information

- Calories: 154 calories
- Total Fat: 9.9 g
- Cholesterol: 0 mg
- Sodium: 184 mg
- Total Carbohydrate: 14.5 g
- Protein: 3.3 g

97. Belas Stuffed Red Bell Peppers

"Red bell peppers are stuffed with a mixture of rice, chard, and black-eyed peas."

Serving: 4 | Prep: 20 m | Cook: 1 h | Ready in: 1 h 20 m

Ingredients

- 1 cup uncooked brown rice
- 2 1/4 cups water
- 4 red bell peppers, tops and seeds removed
- 1 teaspoon olive oil
- 1/4 onion, chopped
- 2 cloves garlic, chopped
- 1 (15 ounce) can black-eyed peas, rinsed and drained
- 2 large Swiss chard leaves, chopped
- salt and black pepper to taste

Direction

- Bring the brown rice and water to a boil in a saucepan over high heat. Reduce the heat to medium-low, cover, and simmer until the rice is tender and the liquid has been absorbed, 45 to 50 minutes.
- Preheat oven to 350 degrees F (175 degrees C). Spray a baking sheet with cooking spray.
- Place the red peppers on the prepared baking sheet, and bake until tender, about 15 minutes.
- Heat the olive oil in a skillet over medium heat, and cook and stir the onion and garlic until the onion is translucent, about 5

minutes. Stir in the black-eyed peas and chard. Bring the mixture to a simmer, and cook until the chard is wilted, 5 to 8 minutes. Mix in the cooked brown rice, sprinkle with salt and pepper to taste, and lightly stuff the mixture into the red peppers. Serve hot.

Nutrition Information

- Calories: 271 calories
- Total Fat: 3.2 g
- Cholesterol: 0 mg
- Sodium: 376 mg
- Total Carbohydrate: 51.4 g
- Protein: 9.5 g

98. Best Ever Cowboy Caviar

"Every time I make this I get asked for the recipe. I keep it on a file in my computer so I can print and email it easily. To add heat it is also good with jalapenos. Serve with tortilla chips."

Serving: 8 | Prep: 15 m | Ready in: 1 d 15 m

Ingredients

- 1/2 cup olive oil
- 1/2 cup vegetable oil
- 1/2 cup cider vinegar
- 1/2 cup white sugar
- 1 (14 ounce) can pinto beans, rinsed and drained
- 1 (14 ounce) can black-eyed peas, rinsed and drained
- 1 (11 ounce) can white shoepeg corn, drained
- 1 red onion, chopped
- 2 stalks celery, chopped
- 1 red bell pepper, chopped
- 1/2 cup chopped cilantro

Direction

- Combine olive oil, vegetable oil, cider vinegar, and sugar in a saucepan; bring to a boil, remove from heat, and cool to room temperature.
- Stir pinto beans, black-eyed peas, corn, onion, celery, red bell pepper, and cilantro together in a large bowl. Pour cooled oil mixture over bean mixture and toss to coat. Cover the bowl with plastic wrap and refrigerate, stirring occasionally, for 24 hours. Drain excess dressing before serving.

Nutrition Information

- Calories: 426 calories
- Total Fat: 28.3 g
- Cholesterol: 0 mg
- Sodium: 415 mg
- Total Carbohydrate: 37.5 g
- Protein: 6.2 g

99. Black Eyed Susan Salad

"Black eyed peas with corn and other veggies with a sweet and sour dressing that keeps getting better the longer it sits."

Serving: 8 | Prep: 20 m | Ready in: 4 h 20 m

Ingredients

- 1 (15 ounce) can black-eyed peas, drained
- 1 (10 ounce) package frozen corn kernels, thawed
- 2 tablespoons chopped pimento peppers
- 1/2 cup chopped celery (optional)
- 2 tablespoons minced onion
- 1/4 cup apple cider vinegar
- 1 tablespoon white sugar
- 2 tablespoons Worcestershire sauce
- 1/2 teaspoon garlic salt
- 1/2 teaspoon pepper
- 1/4 cup vegetable oil

Direction

- Combine the black-eyed peas, corn, pimentos, celery, and onion in a mixing bowl; set aside. In a separate bowl, whisk together the vinegar, sugar, Worcestershire sauce, garlic salt, and pepper. Slowly whisk in the vegetable oil until the dressing emulsifies. Stir the dressing into the vegetables until evenly coated. Refrigerate 4 hours to overnight before serving.

Nutrition Information

- Calories: 146 calories
- Total Fat: 7.4 g
- Cholesterol: 0 mg
- Sodium: 320 mg
- Total Carbohydrate: 17.7 g
- Protein: 3.7 g

100. BlackEyed Pea Bratwurst Stew

"You can make this dish in the slow cooker or simmer on stove. Hearty, inexpensive and easy! Serve with rice or have plenty of bread on hand to soak up the juices!"

Serving: 8 | Prep: 15 m | Cook: 3 h | Ready in: 3 h 15 m

Ingredients

- 2 pounds bratwurst sausages, cut into thirds
- 2 (15 ounce) cans black-eyed peas, rinsed and drained
- 2 (9 ounce) packages frozen cut green beans, thawed
- 2 cups cubed potatoes
- 1 cup chopped onion
- 2 cloves garlic, minced
- 1 (32 fluid ounce) container chicken stock
- 2 tablespoons hot Buffalo wing sauce (such as Frank's® REDHOT Buffalo Wing Sauce), or to taste
- 2 tablespoons ketchup
- 1 tablespoon Worcestershire sauce
- 1/2 teaspoon ground thyme
- salt and ground black pepper to taste
- 1/4 cup all-purpose flour (optional)
- 1 cup water (optional)

Direction

- Place bratwurst sausages, black-eyed peas, green beans, potatoes, onion, garlic, chicken stock, Buffalo wing sauce,

ketchup, Worcestershire sauce, thyme, salt, and black pepper in a slow cooker.
- Cook on High setting until vegetables are tender and soup is thickened, 3 to 4 hours.
- For a thicker stew, whisk flour and water together in a bowl until smooth. Pour mixture into stew and simmer until thickened, about 5 minutes.

Nutrition Information

- Calories: 530 calories
- Total Fat: 32.1 g
- Cholesterol: 69 mg
- Sodium: 1909 mg
- Total Carbohydrate: 37.9 g
- Protein: 21.5 g

101. BlackEyed Pea Gumbo

"A winter time favorite at our house. We always have it for New Year's Day while we watch football! Serve with a tossed salad and corn bread."

Serving: 8 | Prep: 15 m | Cook: 55 m | Ready in: 1 h 10 m

Ingredients

- 1 tablespoon olive oil
- 1 medium onion, chopped
- 1 medium green bell pepper, chopped
- 5 stalks celery, chopped
- 2 cups chicken broth
- 1 cup brown rice
- 4 (15 ounce) cans black-eyed peas with liquid
- 1 (10 ounce) can diced tomatoes and green chiles
- 1 (14.5 ounce) can diced tomatoes
- 2 cloves garlic, finely chopped

Direction

- Heat the olive oil in a large saucepan over medium heat, and cook the onion, pepper, and celery until tender. Pour in the chicken broth, and mix in rice, black-eyed peas with liquid, diced tomatoes and green chiles, diced tomatoes, and garlic. Bring to a boil, reduce heat to low, and simmer 45 minutes, or until rice is tender. Add water if soup is too thick.

Nutrition Information

- Calories: 272 calories

- Total Fat: 3.4 g
- Cholesterol: 0 mg
- Sodium: 870 mg
- Total Carbohydrate: 48.5 g
- Protein: 12.5 g

102. BlackEyed Pea Salad III

"This is an easy, quick, and inexpensive salad to make. Two cans of black-eyed peas, cherry tomatoes, purple onion, and Italian dressing!"

Serving: 8 | Prep: 10 m | Ready in: 1 h 10 m

Ingredients

- 2 (15 ounce) cans black-eyed peas, rinsed and drained
- 1 cup cherry tomatoes, halved
- 1/2 small red onion, cut into slivers
- 1/2 cup light Italian-style salad dressing

Direction

- Lightly mix the black-eyed peas, cherry tomatoes, onion, and salad dressing together in a salad bowl; let stand for 1 hour to blend the flavors before serving.

Nutrition Information

- Calories: 98 calories
- Total Fat: 1.6 g
- Cholesterol: < 1 mg
- Sodium: 521 mg
- Total Carbohydrate: 16.3 g
- Protein: 5.3 g

103. BlackEyed Pea Soup

"This is a great New Year's meal! Perfect on a cold winter night. Great comfort food. Serve with corn bread."

Serving: 8 | Prep: 15 m | Cook: 1 h | Ready in: 1 h 15 m

Ingredients

- 1 pound bulk pork sausage
- 1 pound ground beef
- 1 large onion, diced
- 4 cups water
- 3 (15 ounce) cans black-eyed peas, drained
- 1 (28 ounce) can diced tomatoes
- 1 (10 ounce) can diced tomatoes with green chile peppers (such as RO*TEL®), undrained
- 1 teaspoon Worcestershire sauce
- 3/4 teaspoon garlic salt
- 1/2 teaspoon salt
- 1 (4 ounce) can chopped green chilies
- 4 teaspoons molasses
- 4 beef bouillon cubes
- 1/4 teaspoon ground black pepper
- 1/4 teaspoon ground cumin

Direction

- In a large Dutch oven, cook and stir the pork sausage and ground beef with the onion over medium heat until the meat is no longer pink, 10 to 12 minutes; drain off excess fat. Pour in the water, and stir in black-eyed peas, diced tomatoes,

tomatoes with green chiles, Worcestershire sauce, garlic salt, salt, canned green chilies, molasses, beef bouillon cubes, black pepper, and cumin until thoroughly mixed.
- Bring the soup to a boil, reduce heat to a simmer, cover, and simmer for 45 minutes.

Nutrition Information

- Calories: 416 calories
- Total Fat: 19.9 g
- Cholesterol: 67 mg
- Sodium: 2228 mg
- Total Carbohydrate: 32 g
- Protein: 26.4 g

104. BlackEyed Peas and Tortillas

"Simple, rich, and mildly spicy dish of black-eyed peas served in flour tortillas."

Serving: 4 | Prep: 10 m | Cook: 15 m | Ready in: 25 m

Ingredients

- 1 tablespoon olive oil
- 1/4 cup finely chopped onion
- 1 (15.5 ounce) can black-eyed peas, drained
- 1/2 cup vegetable stock
- 1 fresh jalapeno pepper, chopped
- 1 clove garlic, minced
- 1 tablespoon fresh lime juice
- salt and pepper to taste
- 4 (12 inch) flour tortillas

Direction

- Heat the olive oil in a medium skillet over medium heat, and cook the onion until tender. Mix in the black-eyed peas, vegetable stock, jalapeno, garlic, and lime juice. Season with salt and pepper to taste, and continue cooking until heated through. Wrap the mixture in the tortillas to serve.

Nutrition Information

- Calories: 487 calories
- Total Fat: 13.2 g
- Cholesterol: 0 mg

- Sodium: 1249 mg
- Total Carbohydrate: 76.8 g
- Protein: 15.1 g

105. BlackEyed Peas With Collard Greens and Turnips

"Just a recipe I came up with on a whim. I serve mine with brown rice."

Serving: 4 | Prep: 20 m | Cook: 50 m | Ready in: 9 h 10 m

Ingredients

- 1 cup dried black-eyed peas
- 4 cups water, or as needed to cover
- 1 tablespoon soy margarine
- 1 turnip, peeled and chopped
- 1 bunch collard greens, chopped
- 2 cloves garlic, minced
- 2 tomatoes, chopped
- 1 tablespoon balsamic vinaigrette salad dressing
- 1 tablespoon olive oil (optional)

Direction

- Place black-eyed peas into a large container and cover with several inches of cool water; let stand 8 hours to overnight. Drain and rinse.
- In a large pot, cover black-eyed peas with fresh water. Bring to a boil over high heat, then reduce the heat to medium-low; cover and simmer until peas are tender, 40 to 60 minutes. Drain.
- Heat soy margarine in a skillet over medium heat. Add turnip and collard greens; cook for 2 minutes.

- Stir black-eyed peas, garlic, and tomatoes into collard mixture; cook and stir until collards are tender, about 5 minutes.
- Season with balsamic vinaigrette and olive oil.

Nutrition Information

- Calories: 233 calories
- Total Fat: 8.6 g
- Cholesterol: 0 mg
- Sodium: 142 mg
- Total Carbohydrate: 30.9 g
- Protein: 11.2 g

106. Classic Texas Caviar

"Don't bother with soaking and cooking beans for Classic Texas Caviar - the canned variety works well. But skip the bottled dressing, and take a little extra time to measure your own vinegar, oil and spices."

Serving: 40

Ingredients

- 2 (15.8 ounce) cans black-eyed peas, drained
- 1 (14.5 ounce) can petite diced tomatoes, drained
- 2 fresh medium jalapenos, stemmed, seeded and minced
- 1 small onion, cut into small dice
- 1/2 yellow bell pepper, stemmed, seeded and cut into small dice
- 1/4 cup chopped fresh cilantro
- 6 tablespoons red wine vinegar
- 6 tablespoons olive oil (not extra virgin)
- 1/2 teaspoon salt
- 1/2 teaspoon ground black pepper
- 1/2 teaspoon garlic powder
- 1 teaspoon dried oregano
- 1 1/2 teaspoons ground cumin

Direction

- Mix all ingredients in a medium bowl; cover and refrigerate 2 hours or up to 2 days. Before serving, adjust seasonings to taste, adding extra vinegar, salt and pepper. Transfer to a serving bowl.

Nutrition Information

- Calories: 40 calories
- Total Fat: 2.2 g
- Cholesterol: 0 mg
- Sodium: 112 mg
- Total Carbohydrate: 4 g
- Protein: 1.2 g

107. Cold BlackEyed Peas and Corn

"My husband raves about this! Easy to eat as a salad, but it's yummy with tortilla chips or Fritos®! It's easy to double or triple, and it's really simple to add more ingredients if you have them, like jalapenos. On its own, it's delicious!"

Serving: 4 | Prep: 10 m | Ready in: 10 m

Ingredients

- 1 (15 ounce) can black-eyed peas, drained
- 1 (15.25 ounce) can whole kernel corn, drained
- 1 (4 ounce) jar diced pimento peppers, drained
- 1/4 onion, grated
- 2 cloves garlic, minced
- 1 tablespoon bottled Italian dressing, or to taste
- 1/2 teaspoon ground coriander
- 1/4 teaspoon dried cilantro

Direction

- Mix black-eyed peas, corn, pimento peppers, onion, garlic, Italian dressing, coriander, and cilantro in a large bowl until well combined.

Nutrition Information

- Calories: 191 calories
- Total Fat: 2.8 g
- Cholesterol: 0 mg
- Sodium: 697 mg
- Total Carbohydrate: 37.5 g

- Protein: 8.3 g

108. Cold Corn Salsa

"Delicious with or without tortilla chips!"

Serving: 8 | Prep: 20 m | Cook: 5 m | Ready in: 9 h 25 m

Ingredients

- 1 (15 ounce) can black beans, drained and rinsed
- 1 (15 ounce) can white corn, drained
- 1 (15 ounce) can black-eyed peas, drained
- 1 cup chopped celery
- 1 red bell pepper, chopped
- 1/2 cup sliced green onion
- 1 cup white sugar
- 3/4 cup apple cider vinegar
- 1/2 cup vegetable oil
- 1 teaspoon ground black pepper

Direction

- Combine black beans, corn, black-eyed peas, celery, red bell pepper, and green onion in a large bowl.
- Whisk sugar, vinegar, oil, and black pepper together in a saucepan; bring to a boil until sugar is dissolved, about 5 minutes. Remove from heat and cool.
- Pour cooled dressing over vegetable-bean mixture; stir to coat. Refrigerate for 8 hours or overnight. Drain excess liquid before serving.

Nutrition Information

- Calories: 354 calories
- Total Fat: 14.4 g
- Cholesterol: 0 mg
- Sodium: 488 mg
- Total Carbohydrate: 51.2 g
- Protein: 7.1 g

109. Cowboy Caviar

"Black beans absorb other flavors superbly, so try to leave this for at least 20 minutes before serving to allow the different flavors to blend together."

Serving: 8 | Prep: 20 m | Ready in: 40 m

Ingredients

- 1 (15.5 ounce) can black beans, drained
- 1 (15.5 ounce) can black-eyed peas, drained
- 1 (14.5 ounce) can diced tomatoes, drained
- 2 cups frozen corn kernels, thawed
- 1/2 medium onion, chopped
- 1/4 green bell pepper, finely chopped
- 1/2 cup chopped pickled jalapeno peppers
- 1/2 teaspoon garlic salt
- 1 cup Italian salad dressing
- 3/4 cup chopped cilantro

Direction

- Mix beans, peas, tomatoes, corn, onion, bell pepper, and jalapeno peppers in a large bowl. Season with garlic salt. Add dressing and cilantro; toss to coat. Refrigerate for 20 minutes or until ready to serve.

Nutrition Information

- Calories: 233 calories
- Total Fat: 9.1 g
- Cholesterol: 0 mg

- Sodium: 1255 mg
- Total Carbohydrate: 32.3 g
- Protein: 7.9 g

110. Deep Fried Black Eyed Peas

"Fun, funky and full of flavor! Think 'far out bar goodies' or your next full-fledged addiction. There's a crazy depth to the flavor and a buttery afterburn. Precooking the peas can be done a day in advance, making serving quick and easy. Enjoy!"

Serving: 16 | Prep: 20 m | Cook: 10 m | Ready in: 8 h 30 m

Ingredients

- 1 pound dried black-eyed peas, sorted and rinsed
- 1 onion, cut into large dice
- 2 bay leaves
- 1 jalapeno pepper, seeded and diced
- canola oil for frying
- 2 teaspoons seafood seasoning (such as Old Bay®)
- 1/2 teaspoon kosher salt

Direction

- Place the black-eyed peas into a large container and cover with several inches of cool water; let stand 8 hours to overnight.
- The next day, drain and rinse the peas. Pour in enough water to cover the peas by 3-inches, then stir in the onion, bay leaves, and jalapeno pepper. Bring to a boil, reduce heat to low, and simmer until the peas are tender but not mushy, 40 to 50 minutes. Add more water if needed to keep the peas covered while cooking. Drain the peas in a colander set in the sink, and spread them onto a baking sheet lined with paper towels or dish towels to drain. Discard bay leaves, and refrigerate the peas until ready to fry.

- Heat oil in a deep-fryer or large saucepan to 375 degrees F (190 degrees C).
- Carefully pour about 1 1/2 cups of peas into the hot oil per batch, and fry until crisp, 4 to 7 minutes. Remove the peas, drain on paper towels, and toss the hot peas in a bowl with seafood seasoning and kosher salt. Serve hot.

Nutrition Information

- Calories: 126 calories
- Total Fat: 3.1 g
- Cholesterol: 0 mg
- Sodium: 133 mg
- Total Carbohydrate: 18.5 g
- Protein: 6.9 g

111. Delilahs Wicked Twelve Alarm Chili

"This recipe features 12 different kinds of peppers, including 10 varieties of hot peppers. It's mad, wicked good, but not for the faint of heart. It's extra hot and spicy, just the way I like it! It can be served over macaroni or pasta, or simply eaten by itself"

Serving: 30 | Prep: 1 h | Cook: 3 h 20 m | Ready in: 4 h 20 m

Ingredients

- 1 (20 ounce) can kidney beans, undrained
- 2 (15 ounce) cans chili beans, undrained
- 2 (14 ounce) cans black beans, undrained
- 2 (15.5 ounce) cans black-eyed peas, undrained
- 1 (28 ounce) can diced tomatoes, undrained
- 2 pounds lean ground beef
- 1 pound hot Italian sausage
- 2 large green bell peppers, chopped
- 1 large red bell pepper, chopped
- 6 small yellow onions, chopped
- 1 red onion, chopped
- 6 cloves garlic, minced
- 1 (4 ounce) can sliced jalapeno peppers, finely chopped
- 1 (7 ounce) can chipotle chiles in adobo sauce, finely chopped
- 6 serrano peppers, finely chopped
- 4 orange habanero chili peppers, finely chopped
- 1 banana pepper, seeded and finely chopped
- 3 cherry peppers, finely chopped
- 1 Anaheim pepper, finely chopped
- 4 red Thai chili peppers, finely chopped

- 4 green Thai chili peppers, finely chopped
- 2 tablespoons chili powder, or to taste
- 1 1/2 tablespoons ground cumin
- 3 tablespoons red pepper flakes
- 1/3 envelope taco seasoning mix
- cayenne pepper, or amount to taste
- salt and ground black pepper to taste

Direction

- Place the kidney beans, chili beans, black beans, and black-eyed peas in a large, heavy pot., and simmer over medium heat.
- Place the ground beef and sausage in a skillet over medium-high heat. Cook until crumbly and evenly browned, about 10 minutes. Drain, and stir into the bean mixture.
- Place the red and green bell peppers, yellow and red onions, and garlic on top of the bean and meat mixture. Cover and steam for at least 10 minutes. Stir in the jalapeno, chipotle, serrano, habanero, banana, cherry and Anaheim peppers, red and green Thai chilies, chili powder, cumin, red pepper flakes, and taco seasoning. Season to taste with cayenne pepper, salt, and black pepper. Cover, and simmer over medium heat, stirring occasionally, for 3 hours.

Nutrition Information

- Calories: 215 calories
- Total Fat: 8.5 g
- Cholesterol: 27 mg
- Sodium: 686 mg
- Total Carbohydrate: 22.4 g

- Protein: 13.8 g

112. DownHome BlackEyed Peas

"This country recipe combines black-eyed peas and okra for a down-home country taste. We like to make this recipe in the winter with fried chicken and mashed potatoes."

Serving: 12 | Prep: 20 m | Cook: 1 h 40 m | Ready in: 3 h

Ingredients

- 3 cups dry black-eyed peas
- 12 cups water
- 3 pounds smoked ham hocks
- 1 1/4 cups chopped onion
- 1 cup chopped celery
- 1 teaspoon salt
- 1/8 teaspoon cayenne pepper
- 1 bay leaf
- 1 (10 ounce) package frozen sliced okra, thawed

Direction

- Pick over the peas, rinse them, and place them in a large Dutch oven or soup pot with the water. Bring the beans to a boil for 2 minutes. Remove from heat, cover, and let stand for 1 hour.
- Stir in the ham hocks, onion, celery, salt, cayenne pepper, and bay leaf; bring to a boil, cover the pot, and simmer until the ham hocks are tender, about 1 1/2 hours. Stir in the okra and simmer until tender, 10 to 15 minutes. Remove and discard bay leaf before serving.

Nutrition Information

- Calories: 435 calories
- Total Fat: 24.5 g
- Cholesterol: 77 mg
- Sodium: 277 mg
- Total Carbohydrate: 25.1 g
- Protein: 28.1 g

113. Easy Coconut Rice and BlackEyed Peas

"Inspired by the Caribbean, this recipe uses coconut milk to add flavor to beans and rice. Add a little zing to a healthy brown rice!"

Serving: 5 | Prep: 5 m | Cook: 40 m | Ready in: 45 m

Ingredients

- 1/2 cup coconut milk
- 2 cups water
- 1 (15.5 ounce) can black-eyed peas, drained
- 1 cup brown rice

Direction

- In a saucepan, combine the coconut milk, water and black-eyed peas. Stir in rice. Bring to a boil, cover and reduce heat to low. Simmer until rice has absorbed all of the liquid, about 40 minutes.

Nutrition Information

- Calories: 249 calories
- Total Fat: 6.3 g
- Cholesterol: 0 mg
- Sodium: 267 mg
- Total Carbohydrate: 41.4 g
- Protein: 7.4 g

114. Easy Hoppin John

"An easy week night dinner that my kids love. Have it with a nice salad, and dinner is done. The red pepper should be adjusted to fit your family's taste."

Serving: 8 | Prep: 15 m | Cook: 30 m | Ready in: 45 m

Ingredients

- 1 pound smoked beef sausage, cut into bite-size pieces
- 1 small onion, chopped
- 3 (15 ounce) cans black-eyed peas, rinsed and drained
- 2 (10.75 ounce) cans low sodium chicken stock
- 1 cup water
- 1/2 teaspoon cayenne pepper, or to taste
- 2 cups uncooked instant rice

Direction

- Place the sausage and onion into a large saucepan over medium heat, and cook and stir until the sausage begins to brown, about 10 minutes. Stir in the black-eyed peas, chicken stock, water, and cayenne pepper, and bring to a boil. Stir in the rice, cover, and cook, stirring occasionally, until the rice is tender, 20 to 25 minutes.

Nutrition Information

- Calories: 406 calories
- Total Fat: 16.7 g
- Cholesterol: 39 mg
- Sodium: 1153 mg

- Total Carbohydrate: 44.8 g
- Protein: 18.4 g

115. Fabiennes BlackEyed Crab Cakes

"Black-eyed peas replace the traditional crackers or breadcrumbs in this recipe. The delicate flavor from the peas help bring out the crab's savory taste. There's no need to add lemon juice to these cakes: the zest ties the seasonings together. This is definitely a winning recipe: a must try!"

Serving: 12 | Prep: 20 m | Cook: 20 m | Ready in: 1 h 10 m

Ingredients

- 1 lemon, zested
- 1 teaspoon mustard powder
- 1 teaspoon seafood seasoning (such as Old Bay®)
- 1 teaspoon onion powder
- 1/4 teaspoon cayenne pepper
- 1/3 cup rinsed and drained canned black-eyed peas
- 1 egg
- 1 tablespoon mayonnaise
- 1 (16 ounce) can crab meat, drained and chunked
- 1/3 cup grated Parmesan cheese
- 1 cup panko bread crumbs
- 1/4 cup olive oil

Direction

- Whisk lemon zest, mustard powder, seafood seasoning, onion powder, and cayenne pepper together in a bowl. Add black-eyed peas to lemon zest mixture and smash with a fork until mixture is crumbly. Stir egg and mayonnaise into pea mixture; gently fold in crab meat and Parmesan cheese until combined.

- Form pea mixture into 5-ounce patties. Pour bread crumbs into a shallow bowl and press patties into bread crumbs, coating both sides. Place patties on a plate and refrigerate until chilled, at least 30 minutes.
- Heat olive oil in a skillet over medium heat; fry patties until golden brown, about 4 minutes per side.

Nutrition Information

- Calories: 131 calories
- Total Fat: 7.4 g
- Cholesterol: 51 mg
- Sodium: 277 mg
- Total Carbohydrate: 7.6 g
- Protein: 10.4 g

116. Fiesta Grilled Chicken

"This main dish stars chicken marinated in tequila that's then grilled, and topped with Texas Bean Salsa and splashed with lime juice. Apple juice can be substituted for the tequila if you choose, and the chicken can also be broiled."

Serving: 6 | Prep: 25 m | Cook: 10 m | Ready in: 6 h 35 m

Ingredients

- Texas Bean Salsa:
- 1 (15.5 ounce) can black beans, rinsed and drained
- 1 (15.5 ounce) can black-eyed peas, rinsed and drained
- 1 (15.5 ounce) can whole kernel corn, drained
- 1 small red onion, chopped
- 1/2 cup chopped green bell pepper
- 1 (4.5 ounce) can diced green chilies, drained
- 2 ripe tomatoes, diced and drained
- 1 cup Italian-style salad dressing
- 2 tablespoons chopped fresh cilantro
- 2 cloves garlic, minced
- 1/2 teaspoon garlic salt
- Chicken:
- 6 skinless, boneless chicken breast halves
- 3 limes, juiced
- 1/3 cup tequila
- 3 teaspoons paprika
- 2 teaspoons salt
- 1 teaspoon pepper
- 6 Romaine lettuce leaves
- 6 sprigs cilantro leaves, for garnish (optional)
- 6 lime wedges, for garnish (optional)

Direction

- To make the salsa, mix the black beans, black-eyed peas, corn, red onion, bell pepper, chiles, and tomatoes together in a bowl. Toss vegetables with the Italian dressing, cilantro, garlic, and garlic salt until evenly blended. Cover, and refrigerate 6 hours or overnight.
- Preheat a grill for medium-high heat.
- About 45 minutes before serving time, place the chicken breasts in a baking dish and drizzle with lime juice and tequila. Sprinkle evenly with paprika, salt, and pepper. Cover the dish, refrigerate, and allow to marinate 10 minutes.
- Remove chicken breasts from the marinade, and discard remaining marinade.
- Cook the chicken breasts on the preheated grill until the juices run clear and the meat is no longer pink, 10 to 12 minutes.
- To serve, place a lettuce leaf on each plate. Top with a chicken breast, and spoon Texas Bean Salsa over each, dividing evenly among servings. If desired, garnish with additional cilantro leaves and lime wedges.

Nutrition Information

- Calories: 512 calories
- Total Fat: 15.8 g
- Cholesterol: 67 mg
- Sodium: 2600 mg
- Total Carbohydrate: 56.4 g
- Protein: 36.4 g

117. Fried BlackEye Peas

"I make these with leftover cooked black-eyed peas cooked with ham hocks or smoked turkey from New Year's. I sometimes top with a fried green tomato or left over candied yams. Get creative with them. I've tried several variations. This is the basic version."

Serving: 4 | Prep: 10 m | Cook: 20 m | Ready in: 30 m

Ingredients

- 1/2 pound bacon
- 3 cups canned black-eyed peas, rinsed and drained
- 2 tablespoons minced shallot
- 1/3 cup chopped roasted red peppers
- 3 tablespoons all-purpose flour, or as needed
- salt and black pepper to taste
- 1 tablespoon butter
- 1 tablespoon vegetable oil

Direction

- Place the bacon in a large, deep skillet, and cook over medium-high heat, turning occasionally, until evenly browned, about 10 minutes. Drain the bacon slices on a paper towel-lined plate.
- Mash the black-eye peas in a bowl with a fork. Crumble the bacon into the peas, and stir in the shallot, red peppers, and enough flour to make the mixture stick together. Season to taste with salt and pepper. Form the black-eye pea mixture into 4 patties.
- Melt the butter with the vegetable oil in a large skillet over medium heat. Cook the patties until golden brown and crispy

on each side, about 4 minutes per side.

Nutrition Information

- Calories: 325 calories
- Total Fat: 15.2 g
- Cholesterol: 28 mg
- Sodium: 1051 mg
- Total Carbohydrate: 31.1 g
- Protein: 16.4 g

118. GlutenFree BlackEyed Pea and Cauliflower Soup

"Great way to bring in good luck with the New Years' tradition of eating black-eyed peas!"

Serving: 8 | Prep: 15 m | Cook: 49 m | Ready in: 1 h 14 m

Ingredients

- 1/2 pound bacon, sliced into small pieces
- 1 tablespoon olive oil
- 1 large white onion, chopped
- 2 tablespoons minced garlic
- 1 teaspoon dried thyme
- 1/2 cup white wine
- 8 cups chicken broth
- 2 (19 ounce) cans black-eyed peas, rinsed and drained
- 1 head cauliflower, broken into small florets
- 1/2 teaspoon ground black pepper

Direction

- Place bacon in a large pot and cook over medium heat, turning occasionally, until evenly browned, about 10 minutes. Drain bacon pieces on paper towels.
- Heat olive oil over medium heat in the same pot. Add onion, garlic, and thyme; cook and stir until onion is softened, about 10 minutes. Stir in wine; cook until slightly reduced, about 4 minutes. Add chicken broth, black-eyed peas, and cauliflower florets. Season with black pepper. Bring to a boil. Reduce heat,

cover, and simmer soup until flavors combine, about 20 minutes.
- Remove soup from heat and let cool briefly, about 10 minutes. Puree soup with an immersion blender until smooth. Top with bacon pieces.

Nutrition Information

- Calories: 226 calories
- Total Fat: 6.9 g
- Cholesterol: 15 mg
- Sodium: 1599 mg
- Total Carbohydrate: 26.3 g
- Protein: 12.6 g

119. Guyanese Cookup Rice

"My grandmother's recipe. It's delicious and can be made with or without meat. It's also very versatile. Here I am using chicken, however you can use brisket, pigtail, oxtail, the list is endless."

Serving: 8 | Prep: 20 m | Cook: 45 m | Ready in: 1 h 5 m

Ingredients

- 1 scotch bonnet chile pepper
- 6 bone-in chicken pieces, such as breasts, thighs, and drumsticks
- 2 skinless, bone-in chicken breast halves - cut in half
- 1 tablespoon olive oil
- 1 onion, finely chopped
- 3 cloves garlic, minced
- 2 cups uncooked long-grain white rice
- 4 cups chicken broth
- 1 (14 ounce) can coconut milk
- 4 sprigs thyme, chopped
- 1 (15 ounce) can black-eyed peas, rinsed and drained
- 4 green onions, coarsely chopped
- 1/2 head cabbage, cored and cut into large chunks
- 2 tablespoons butter
- salt and pepper to taste

Direction

- Slice the scotch bonnet chile in half, and chop one half. Reserve both halves. (Chile is very hot, so use gloves when

chopping, and avoid touching your eyes, nose, or mouth after chopping.) Cut the chicken pieces into large chunks.
- Heat the olive oil in a large skillet or Dutch oven over medium heat, and pan-fry the chicken pieces until brown on all sides, about 15 minutes. Stir in chopped chile, onion, and garlic. Cook, stirring occasionally, until the onion is translucent, about 5 minutes. Add the rice, and stir to coat with oil. Let the rice fry until it turns slightly opaque but doesn't brown. Pour in the chicken stock, bring to a boil over medium heat, and reduce heat to a simmer. Let the mixture simmer for about 5 minutes, and stir in the coconut milk, thyme, black-eyed peas, and green onions until well combined. Lay the cabbage chunks on top of the mixture, and place the remaining half chile on top of the cabbage.
- Cover, and simmer until the rice and cabbage are tender, about 20 minutes. Check occasionally to see if the mixture is getting too dry on the bottom, and add a small amount of water if needed to prevent burning. Before serving, stir in butter, and season to taste with salt and pepper.

Nutrition Information

- Calories: 541 calories
- Total Fat: 23.8 g
- Cholesterol: 68 mg
- Sodium: 255 mg
- Total Carbohydrate: 55.6 g
- Protein: 26.7 g

120. Hawg Wild BlackEyed Peas

"This is my own variation on the traditional New Year's meal, but really takes it up a notch. I usually end up making it a lot each winter. If word gets out to friends that I'm making this, I don't have leftovers. Serve with corn bread. I sometimes use some of the hog jowl instead of bacon. Slice it thin and then chop into small pieces, and just leave it in the pan while cooking the Trinity (onion, celery, and bell pepper)."

Serving: 16 | Prep: 30 m | Cook: 3 h 50 m | Ready in: 12 h 20 m

Ingredients

- 2 pounds dried black-eyed peas
- 1 1/2 pounds smoked pork jowl, cut into 4 pieces
- 1 pound tasso ham, cut into 1/2-inch pieces
- 1 onion, chopped
- 1 stalk celery
- 2 cloves garlic, minced
- 3 bay leaves
- 1 tablespoon dried parsley
- 1 tablespoon dried basil
- 1 tablespoon Worcestershire sauce
- 8 strips bacon
- 2 cups chopped onion
- 2 cups chopped celery
- 2 cups chopped green bell pepper
- 3 cloves garlic, minced
- 2 (10 ounce) cans diced tomatoes with green chile peppers (such as RO*TEL®), drained
- 1 1/2 pounds smoked andouille sausage, sliced on the bias
- 1 1/2 tablespoons white sugar
- salt and ground black pepper to taste

Direction

- Place black-eyed peas into a large bowl and cover with several inches of cool water; soak 8 hours to overnight. Drain and rinse.
- Place black-eyed peas into a large pot and fill with water 1/2-inch above the peas; bring to a simmer. Add pork jowl, tasso ham, 1 chopped onion, 1 stalk celery, 2 cloves minced garlic, bay leaves, parsley, basil, and Worcestershire sauce; cook at a simmer until peas are tender, 2 to 3 hours.
- Remove and discard pork jowl, celery stalk, and bay leaves from the pea mixture.
- Cook bacon in a large skillet over medium-high heat, turning occasionally, until evenly browned, about 10 minutes. Drain bacon slices on paper towels, leaving 2 to 3 tablespoons bacon drippings in the skillet. Crumble bacon when cooled.
- Cook and stir 2 cups onion, 2 cups celery, green bell pepper, and 3 cloves garlic in the hot bacon drippings over medium heat until onion is tender, about 10 minutes.
- Mix onion mixture, tomatoes with green chiles, bacon, and andouille sausage into pea mixture. Season with sugar, salt, and pepper. Simmer pea mixture until flavors have blended, 1 1/2 hours.

Nutrition Information

- Calories: 712 calories
- Total Fat: 48 g
- Cholesterol: 81 mg
- Sodium: 947 mg
- Total Carbohydrate: 42.2 g
- Protein: 28.6 g

121. Hearty Hoppin John Stew

"I couldn't find a Hoppin' John recipe I really cared for, so I threw this together to enjoy black-eyed peas for New Year's."

Serving: 4 | Prep: 20 m | Cook: 1 h 20 m | Ready in: 1 h 40 m

Ingredients

- 1/2 pound bulk pork sausage
- 1 stalk celery, sliced
- 1 small onion, chopped
- 3 cloves garlic, minced
- 1/2 red bell pepper, diced
- 3/4 cup brown and wild rice mix
- 1 (15 ounce) can black-eyed peas, drained and rinsed
- 1 (14.5 ounce) can diced tomatoes with juice
- 2 1/3 cups chicken stock
- 1 tablespoon Cajun seasoning, or more to taste
- salt to taste
- freshly cracked black pepper to taste

Direction

- Cook and stir sausage in a large skillet over medium heat until meat is still slightly pink, about 8 minutes. Mix celery and onion into sausage; cook and stir until onion is translucent, about 5 more minutes. Stir garlic and red bell pepper into sausage mixture and cook until bell pepper is slightly soft, about 5 minutes.
- Stir brown and wild rice mix, black-eyed peas, tomatoes with their juice, chicken stock, and Cajun seasoning into sausage

and vegetables. Bring to a boil, reduce heat to low, and cover; simmer 45 minutes. Remove cover, raise heat to medium-low, and simmer until stew is thickened, about 15 minutes. Season with salt and cracked black pepper.

Nutrition Information

- Calories: 354 calories
- Total Fat: 13.8 g
- Cholesterol: 33 mg
- Sodium: 1868 mg
- Total Carbohydrate: 39.2 g
- Protein: 16.8 g

122. Italian Hot Turkey Sausage and BlackEyed Peas

"This easy dish was a big surprise. My husband rated it 9 out of 10 food stars."

Serving: 6 | Prep: 20 m | Cook: 35 m | Ready in: 55 m

Ingredients

- 2 tablespoons extra-virgin olive oil
- 1 small yellow onion, chopped
- 2 stalks celery, thinly sliced
- 3 cloves garlic, minced
- 2 teaspoons dried oregano
- 6 hot Italian turkey sausage links, skinned and coarsely chopped
- 1 (14.5 ounce) can no-salt-added diced tomatoes
- 1 (15 ounce) can black-eyed peas, rinsed and drained
- 2 (14 ounce) cans canned low-sodium chicken broth
- 8 ounces whole wheat thin spaghetti, broken into 3-inch pieces
- 1/4 cup grated Parmesan cheese

Direction

- Heat the olive oil in a large skillet over medium heat; cook and stir the onion and celery in the hot oil until softened, about 3 minutes. Stir in the garlic and oregano, let cook for 1 more minute. Push the cooked ingredients to the sides of the pan. Cook sausage meat in the center of the pan until no longer pink, about 5 minutes.

- Stir in the tomatoes, black-eyed peas, and chicken broth. Cover the skillet and reduce heat to medium-low. Let the mixture simmer until the vegetables are tender and the meat is thoroughly cooked, stirring occasionally, 18 to 20 minutes. Mix in the broken spaghetti and let the mixture cook until the pasta is tender, 6 to 8 minutes. Ladle into a heated serving bowl and sprinkle with Parmesan cheese.

Nutrition Information

- Calories: 428 calories
- Total Fat: 17.1 g
- Cholesterol: 73 mg
- Sodium: 1238 mg
- Total Carbohydrate: 39.8 g
- Protein: 30 g

123. Kala BlackEyed Pea Fritters from the Dutch Antilles

"These spicy fritters made from black eyed peas are originally from the Dutch Antilles, a group of five small islands in the Caribbean."

Serving: 10 | Prep: 15 m | Cook: 5 m | Ready in: 12 h 20 m

Ingredients

- 2 cups dried black-eyed peas
- 2 egg whites
- 1 teaspoon salt
- 1/2 cup all-purpose flour
- 1 teaspoon cayenne pepper, or to taste
- vegetable oil for deep frying

Direction

- Place black-eyed peas into a container, and cover with several inches of water. Allow to stand for 12 hours.
- Drain the water from the black-eyed peas. Place peas into the bowl of a food processor, and pulse until coarsely ground. Stir in the egg whites, salt, flour, and cayenne pepper to taste until dough consistency. Add more flour if necessary to hold the mixture together. Form into small balls, each about 2 inches diameter.
- Heat the oil in a heavy, deep skillet to 375 degrees F (190 degrees C) over medium-high heat. Carefully drop the balls into the hot oil, and fry until brown, about 5 minutes. You may need

to lower the heat slightly after cooking the first kala balls. Turn frequently to brown evenly on all sides.

Nutrition Information

- Calories: 217 calories
- Total Fat: 9.3 g
- Cholesterol: 0 mg
- Sodium: 249 mg
- Total Carbohydrate: 25 g
- Protein: 9.3 g

124. Loaded Blackeyed Peas Spinach and Vegetable Soup

"An easy, filling, and hearty vegan alternative to the traditional New Year's Day black-eyed pea recipes."

Serving: 10 | Prep: 30 m | Cook: 1 h 40 m | Ready in: 2 h 10 m

Ingredients

- 1 tablespoon olive oil, or as needed
- 1 large onion, chopped
- 4 cloves garlic, crushed
- 6 cups vegetable broth
- 3 potatoes, cubed
- 1 1/2 cups dry black-eyed peas
- 3 carrots, sliced
- 1 zucchini, peeled and cubed
- 1 (10 ounce) bag fresh spinach, stems removed
- 1 tablespoon chopped fresh parsley
- 2 bay leaves
- salt and ground black pepper to taste

Direction

- Heat olive oil in a large pot or Dutch oven over medium heat; cook and stir onion and garlic in the hot oil until lightly browned, about 10 minutes. Add vegetable broth and bring to a boil.
- Mix potatoes, black-eyed peas, carrots, zucchini, spinach, parsley, and bay leaves into the broth. Season with salt and black pepper. Bring to a boil, reduce heat, and simmer soup

until peas are tender and flavors have blended, 1 1/2 to 2 hours.

Nutrition Information

- Calories: 177 calories
- Total Fat: 2.2 g
- Cholesterol: 0 mg
- Sodium: 322 mg
- Total Carbohydrate: 32.5 g
- Protein: 8.1 g

125. Lucky Pea Soup

"This delicious black-eyed pea soup is a favorite of ours especially when the weather is chilly. It's a great way to start the year with a kicked-up, spicy serving of black-eyed peas! Top with shredded cheese, parsley, green onions, and crumbled bacon to add even more flavor. "

Serving: 4 | Prep: 15 m | Cook: 40 m | Ready in: 55 m

Ingredients

- 4 slices bacon
- 1 green bell pepper, chopped
- 1 small onion, chopped
- 2 (15 ounce) cans black-eyed peas, undrained
- 2 (14.5 ounce) cans diced tomatoes, undrained
- 1 cup water
- 1 1/2 teaspoons salt
- 1 1/4 teaspoons cumin
- 1 1/4 teaspoons dry mustard
- 1 teaspoon chili powder
- 1/2 teaspoon curry powder
- 1/2 teaspoon pepper
- 1/2 teaspoon sugar

Direction

- Place the bacon in a skillet and cook over medium-high heat until crisp and evenly brown. Drain on paper towels. When cool, crumble into small pieces.
- Using the same skillet, add the peppers and onion; stir and cook over medium-high heat until transparent and tender, about

5 minutes.
- Pour the black beans, tomatoes, and water into a large pot. Stir in the peppers, onion, salt, cumin, dry mustard, chili powder, curry powder, pepper, and sugar. Bring to a boil, reduce heat to medium, cover, and simmer 20 to 25 minutes. Serve hot sprinkled with bacon, and other toppings of your choice.

Nutrition Information

- Calories: 272 calories
- Total Fat: 6 g
- Cholesterol: 10 mg
- Sodium: 1745 mg
- Total Carbohydrate: 41.6 g
- Protein: 16 g

126. Melissas BlackEyed Pea Salad

"Perfect for New Year's Day."

Serving: 4 | Prep: 15 m | Ready in: 8 h 15 m

Ingredients

- 1 1/2 cups canned black-eyed peas, rinsed and drained
- 3/4 cup diced green bell pepper
- 1/2 cup diced celery
- 1/2 cup diced red onion
- 1/4 cup diced yellow onion
- 1/4 cup vegetable oil
- 1/4 cup white sugar
- 2 tablespoons apple cider vinegar
- 1 clove garlic, minced
- 1/2 teaspoon salt
- 1/2 teaspoon ground black pepper
- 1/2 teaspoon hot pepper sauce (optional)

Direction

- Combine black-eyed peas, green bell pepper, celery, red onion, and yellow onion in a large bowl.
- Whisk vegetable oil, sugar, cider vinegar, garlic, salt, black pepper, and hot pepper sauce together in a bowl.
- Pour vinegar mixture over vegetables; toss to coat. Cover and refrigerate overnight before serving.

Nutrition Information

- Calories: 262 calories
- Total Fat: 14.2 g
- Cholesterol: 0 mg
- Sodium: 578 mg
- Total Carbohydrate: 29.9 g
- Protein: 5 g

127. Moms PurpleHull Peas

"A wonderful side-dish for any southern-style-meal. Goes great with cornbread and fried pork chops!"

Serving: 6 | Prep: 10 m | Cook: 2 h | Ready in: 2 h 10 m

Ingredients

- 1 1/2 pounds frozen purple hull peas
- 8 ounces fresh okra (optional)
- 4 ounces bacon, cut into 1/2 inch pieces
- 1 tablespoon white sugar
- 1/8 teaspoon baking soda
- salt and pepper to taste

Direction

- Place the purple hull peas into a large pot and cover with water. Bring to a boil over high heat, add okra if using and boil for 2 minutes, stirring twice. Reduce heat to medium-low, add the bacon, sugar, baking soda, salt, and pepper. Cover and simmer until tender, 1 1/2 to 2 hours.

Nutrition Information

- Calories: 194 calories
- Total Fat: 9.2 g
- Cholesterol: 13 mg
- Sodium: 526 mg
- Total Carbohydrate: 20.3 g
- Protein: 8.3 g

128. My Hoppin John

"More stew than soup, it's a classic New Year's Day meal! I couldn't find a recipe that had everything I liked, so I took 4 different ones and combined parts to make it all my own. Served it to friends this New Year's Day with fresh baked bread and they all loved it (even the kids)! I used the ham bone and scrap ham from the leftover Christmas ham."

Serving: 8 | Prep: 30 m | Cook: 50 m | Ready in: 1 h 30 m

Ingredients

- 1 tablespoon olive oil
- 1 large meaty ham bone
- 1 1/2 cups chopped onion
- 3 stalks celery, chopped
- 2 cloves garlic, minced
- 3 (15 ounce) cans black-eyed peas, rinsed and drained
- 2 cups water
- 1 1/4 cups chicken broth, or more as needed
- 1 cup dry white wine
- 1 cup chopped ham
- 2 bay leaves
- 1/4 teaspoon dried thyme
- salt and pepper to taste
- 2 cups uncooked white rice
- 4 cups water

Direction

- Heat the olive oil in a large Dutch oven or soup pot over medium-high heat and brown the ham bone on all sides, about 15 minutes. Reduce heat to medium and stir in the onion,

celery, and garlic, and cook until the onion is translucent, stirring often, about 5 minutes. Add the black-eyed peas, 2 cups of water, chicken broth, wine, ham, bay leaves, thyme, salt, and pepper; stir. Bring the mixture to a boil. Reduce heat and simmer until the mixture is thickened and the flavors have blended, 30 to 60 minutes. Add more chicken stock if the mixture is too thick.
- About 30 minutes before serving, bring the rice and 4 cups of water to a boil in a saucepan. Reduce heat to medium-low, cover, and simmer until the rice is tender and the liquid has been absorbed, 20 to 25 minutes. Let the rice stand covered for about 10 minutes to absorb steam.
- Remove the ham bone from the soup, cutting any extra ham off the bone and returning it to the pot. Discard the bone. Stir the cooked rice into the black-eyed pea mixture until well combined and serve.

Nutrition Information

- Calories: 399 calories
- Total Fat: 6.1 g
- Cholesterol: 9 mg
- Sodium: 709 mg
- Total Carbohydrate: 64.9 g
- Protein: 14.8 g

129. Press Box Vegetable Salsa Dip

"Great vegetable-bean dip for any party or appetizer event. Serve with scoop chips or any tortilla chip you like. Enjoy!"

Serving: 15 | Prep: 15 m | Ready in: 3 h 15 m

Ingredients

- 1 (15.5 ounce) can yellow hominy, drained
- 1 (15.5 ounce) can white hominy, drained
- 1 (15 ounce) can black-eyed peas, drained
- 1/2 cup chopped onion
- 1/2 cup chopped red bell pepper
- 1/2 cup chopped, seeded tomato
- 1 clove garlic, finely chopped
- 1 (8 ounce) bottle zesty Italian-style salad dressing

Direction

- Mix yellow hominy, white hominy, black-eyed peas, onion, red bell pepper, tomato, and garlic together in a bowl. Stir Italian-style dressing into the mixture. Allow to marinate in refrigerator for 3 hours.

Nutrition Information

- Calories: 112 calories
- Total Fat: 4.9 g
- Cholesterol: 0 mg
- Sodium: 452 mg
- Total Carbohydrate: 14.8 g

- Protein: 2.4 g

130. Pressure Cooked BlackEyed Peas with Smoked Turkey Leg

"The title says it all. A wonderful combination of black-eyed peas, turkey, and seasonings. It takes less than 1 hour to make these tasty beans in your pressure cooker."

Serving: 10 | Prep: 10 m | Cook: 25 m | Ready in: 45 m

Ingredients

- 2 pounds dried black-eyed peas, sorted and rinsed
- 1 large smoked turkey leg
- 1 onion, chopped
- 2 cloves garlic, chopped, or to taste
- olive oil
- 1 teaspoon ground black pepper, or to taste

Direction

- Place peas and turkey leg into a pressure cooker. Stir in onion, garlic, olive oil, pepper, and water to cover. Bring to a simmer. Close and lock lid.
- Adjust temperature until regulator is gently rocking. Cook at high pressure for 15 to 20 minutes. Let pressure release naturally according to manufacturer's instructions for at least 5 minutes; open lid and add more water if needed. Replace lid and cook until beans are tender, 5 to 15 minutes more. Let pressure cooker cool for about 5 minutes before opening. Remove turkey bone.

Nutrition Information

- Calories: 451 calories
- Total Fat: 5.6 g
- Cholesterol: 61 mg
- Sodium: 71 mg
- Total Carbohydrate: 55.9 g
- Protein: 45 g

131. Quick Coconut Curry with Rice Corn and Beans

"This is a quick curry because there are no vegetables to clean and chop. All ingredients are ones that can be stored on the shelf or freezer."

Serving: 7 | Prep: 15 m | Cook: 20 m | Ready in: 35 m

Ingredients

- 1 (15 ounce) can black-eyed peas, undrained
- 1 (14 ounce) can coconut milk
- 1/2 (12 ounce) package frozen corn
- 1 (5.5 ounce) can tomato paste
- 2 tablespoons Jamaican-style curry powder
- 1 tablespoon white sugar
- 3/4 teaspoon salt, or to taste
- 4 cups water, or as needed
- 1 3/4 cups basmati rice
- 1 pinch salt

Direction

- Mix black-eyed peas, coconut milk, corn, tomato paste, curry powder, sugar, and 3/4 teaspoon salt in a pot until smooth and evenly combined; simmer over medium-low heat, stirring often, until curry sauce is heated through, about 5 minutes.
- Pour enough water into a separate pot to almost fill and bring to a boil; season with a pinch of salt. Add rice to boiling water and cook, stirring occasionally, until rice is very soft, about 15 minutes. Drain excess water from rice.

- Mix rice and curry sauce together in a large bowl.

Nutrition Information

- Calories: 374 calories
- Total Fat: 13.4 g
- Cholesterol: 0 mg
- Sodium: 615 mg
- Total Carbohydrate: 58.6 g
- Protein: 9.4 g

132. Quick Corn and Bean Salsa

"If you want a different type of salsa than your standard salsa, this is the one for you. Great for potlucks and will have everyone asking for more. Chill and serve with tortilla chips."

Serving: 20 | Prep: 15 m | Ready in: 35 m

Ingredients

- 1 (15.25 ounce) can yellow corn, drained
- 1 (15.25 ounce) can white corn, drained
- 1 (15 ounce) can black beans, rinsed and drained
- 1 (15 ounce) can black-eyed peas, rinsed and drained
- 3 tomatoes, diced
- 2 avocados - peeled, pitted, and cut into small cubes
- 1 bunch cilantro, chopped
- 7 green onions, chopped
- 1 (16 ounce) bottle zesty Italian-style salad dressing

Direction

- Mix yellow corn, white corn, black beans, black-eyed peas, tomatoes, avocados, cilantro, and green onion together in a large mixing bowl. Pour salad dressing over the corn mixture and stir to coat.
- Cover bowl with plastic wrap and refrigerate until chilled, at least 20 minutes.

Nutrition Information

- Calories: 173 calories

- Total Fat: 9.9 g
- Cholesterol: 0 mg
- Sodium: 642 mg
- Total Carbohydrate: 19.8 g
- Protein: 4.2 g

133. Spicy Bean Salsa

"Serve with tortilla chips. Very addicting!"

Serving: 12 | Prep: 10 m | Ready in: 8 h 10 m

Ingredients

- 1 (15 ounce) can black-eyed peas
- 1 (15 ounce) can black beans, rinsed and drained
- 1 (15 ounce) can whole kernel corn, drained
- 1/2 cup chopped onion
- 1/2 cup chopped green bell pepper
- 1 (4 ounce) can diced jalapeno peppers
- 1 (14.5 ounce) can diced tomatoes, drained
- 1 cup Italian-style salad dressing
- 1/2 teaspoon garlic salt

Direction

- In a medium bowl, combine black-eyed peas, black beans, corn, onion, green bell pepper, jalapeno peppers and tomatoes. Season with Italian-style salad dressing and garlic salt; mix well. Cover, and refrigerate overnight to blend flavors.

Nutrition Information

- Calories: 155 calories
- Total Fat: 6.4 g
- Cholesterol: 0 mg
- Sodium: 949 mg

- Total Carbohydrate: 20.4 g
- Protein: 5 g

134. Spicy BlackEyed Pea Soup

"This is a wonderful spicy and flavorful soup. Perfect for a crisp fall day. It is incredibly easy too and goes great with corn bread!"

Serving: 12 | Prep: 10 m | Cook: 55 m | Ready in: 1 h 5 m

Ingredients

- 1 pound bacon, diced
- 1 cup chopped white onion
- 2 tablespoons diced fresh jalapeno pepper
- 1 clove garlic, minced
- 4 (15 ounce) cans black-eyed peas, undrained
- 3 cups water
- 2 cups canned diced tomatoes
- 2 cubes beef bouillon
- 3 cups shredded Cheddar cheese

Direction

- Cook and stir bacon in a stockpot over medium heat until slightly browned, 5 to 10 minutes. Add onion, jalapeno pepper, and garlic; cook until bacon is slightly crisp, 5 to 10 more minutes. Add black-eyed peas, water, tomatoes, and beef bouillon; bring to a low boil.
- Reduce heat and simmer, stirring frequently, until flavors have blended, about 30 minutes. Add Cheddar cheese and continue to cook, stirring frequently, until cheese is melted, about 15 minutes.

Nutrition Information

- Calories: 303 calories
- Total Fat: 15.4 g
- Cholesterol: 43 mg
- Sodium: 1084 mg
- Total Carbohydrate: 22.7 g
- Protein: 18.9 g

135. Spinach and Bean Casserole

"This is one of my favorite recipes, tasty and genuine. I hope you all enjoy it."

Serving: 4 | Prep: 5 m | Cook: 45 m | Ready in: 50 m

Ingredients

- 1 cup dry black-eyed peas
- 1/4 cup olive oil
- 1 onion, chopped
- 3 cups fresh spinach
- 1 (28 ounce) can peeled and diced tomatoes
- 2 teaspoons salt
- 1 teaspoon fennel seed, ground

Direction

- Preheat oven to 350 degrees F (175 degrees C).
- Cook black-eye peas in a pressure cooker for 12 minutes.
- Heat oil in a large saucepan over medium high heat. Sauté onion with spinach, tomatoes, salt and fennel for 15 minutes.
- Combine beans with spinach mixture in a 2 quart casserole dish.
- Bake in preheated oven for 15 minutes.

Nutrition Information

- Calories: 282 calories
- Total Fat: 14.2 g
- Cholesterol: 0 mg

- Sodium: 1707 mg
- Total Carbohydrate: 28.7 g
- Protein: 9.7 g

136. Spinach Salad with Hot Bacon Dressing

"This spinach salad with black-eyed peas is a twist on one of my favorite culinary traditions: serving beans and greens on New Year's Day. Greens represent paper money and beans symbolize coins. Here I present these ingredients in salad form, which is a great delivery system for hot bacon dressing."

Serving: 6 | Prep: 15 m | Cook: 15 m | Ready in: 30 m

Ingredients

- 1/2 pound sliced bacon, cut crosswise into 1/2-inch strips
- 1/4 cup vegetable oil
- 1/2 cup minced onion
- 1 pinch salt
- 2 cloves garlic, minced
- 1/3 cup apple cider vinegar
- 1/4 cup rice vinegar
- 1/2 cup water
- 1/2 cup white sugar
- 1 1/2 tablespoons Dijon mustard
- 1/3 cup bacon drippings
- 2 teaspoons water
- 1 teaspoon cornstarch
- 1 pinch cayenne pepper
- salt and ground black pepper to taste
- 1 pound baby spinach leaves
- 1 (15 ounce) can black-eyed peas, rinsed and drained
- 12 white button mushrooms, thinly sliced
- 1 cup sliced cherry tomatoes

Direction

- Cook and stir bacon with 1/4 cup vegetable in a skillet over medium heat until bacon is browned and crisp, 5 to 7 minutes. Pour bacon into a strainer set over a bowl, reserving 1/3 cup of bacon drippings.
- Return skillet to medium heat. Stir onions and salt into the skillet; cook and stir until onions are golden brown, about 5 minutes. Stir in garlic; cook, stirring constantly, until the garlic is fragrant and golden, 1 minute.
- Stir cider vinegar, rice vinegar, 1/2 cup water, sugar, and Dijon mustard into onion mixture. Increase heat to medium-high and simmer.
- Whisk 2 teaspoons water and cornstarch in a bowl. Gradually pour cornstarch mixture into onion mixture and whisk until thickened. 3 to 4 minutes. Reduce heat to low.
- Drizzle reserved 1/3 cup bacon drippings into onion mixture, whisking constantly. Add cooked bacon and stir to combine. Season with cayenne pepper, salt, and black pepper to taste.
- Combine spinach, black-eyed peas, mushrooms, and cherry tomatoes in a large bowl; toss to combine. Drizzle hot bacon dressing over spinach mixture; toss quickly and serve immediately.

Nutrition Information

- Calories: 430 calories
- Total Fat: 28.3 g
- Cholesterol: 26 mg
- Sodium: 674 mg
- Total Carbohydrate: 34.4 g
- Protein: 11.6 g

137. Super Bean Pie

"For the legume fanatic, have this for dessert or as a side. A major bean infusion pour into a nutty crust. WARNING: Soak the beans to release any gassy properties."

Serving: 8 | Prep: 20 m | Cook: 45 m | Ready in: 10 h 15 m

Ingredients

- 2 1/2 cups all-purpose flour (spooned and leveled), plus more for rolling and cutting out dough
- 2 tablespoons white sugar
- 1 teaspoon salt
- 1 cup vegetable shortening, chilled
- 1 1/2 cups butter
- 6 tablespoons ice water
- 1/2 cup dried great Northern beans, soaked overnight
- 1/2 cup dry garbanzo beans, soaked overnight
- 1/2 cup dry navy beans, soaked overnight
- 1/2 cup dry black beans, soaked overnight
- 1/2 cup dried black-eyed peas, soaked overnight
- 1/2 cup dry mixed lentils, soaked overnight
- 1/2 cup dried pinto beans, soaked overnight
- 1/2 cup dry kidney beans, soaked overnight
- 1/4 cup olive oil
- 1/2 cup prepared hummus
- 1 teaspoon ground nutmeg
- 1 teaspoon ground ginger
- 1 teaspoon ground cinnamon
- 1 teaspoon ground allspice
- 1/2 teaspoon cream of tartar
- 1 tablespoon vanilla extract

Direction

- Whisk together the flour, sugar, and salt in a mixing bowl. Cut in the chilled shortening and butter with a knife or pastry blender until the mixture resembles coarse crumbs. (This can also be done in a food processor: pulse the cold shortening and butter until it's the size of small peas. Turn mixture into a bowl and proceed.) Add the ice water a tablespoon at a time, tossing with a fork, until the flour mixture is moistened. Do not add more water than you need: when you squeeze a handful of the moistened pastry mixture, it should form a ball. Divide the dough in half and shape into balls. Wrap in plastic and refrigerate for at least 1 hour or up to three days. Roll one ball out to fit a 9 inch pie plate. Place bottom crust in pie plate and chill for at least 20 minutes before baking. Roll out top crust and set aside.
- Preheat an oven to 350 degrees F (175 degrees C).
- Drain the great Northern beans, garbanzo beans, navy beans, black beans, black-eyed peas, lentils, pinto beans, and kidney beans and place in a food processor. Blend beans while slowly drizzling the olive oil into the mixture. Blend in the hummus. Pour the batter into a large mixing bowl and stir in the nutmeg, ginger, cinnamon, allspice, cream of tartar, and vanilla extract. Pour the batter into the pie crust and smooth with a spatula. Place the second pie crust on top. Seal the edges using a fork.
- Bake in the preheated oven until a knife inserted into the center comes out clean, about 45 minutes. Cool in the pans for 10 minutes before removing to cool completely on a wire rack.

Nutrition Information

- Calories: 1078 calories

- Total Fat: 70 g
- Cholesterol: 92 mg
- Sodium: 644 mg
- Total Carbohydrate: 90.1 g
- Protein: 25.1 g

138. Sweet and Sour BlackEyed Peas

"This has become my new go-to recipe for black-eyed peas. I'm a Southern girl and never thought I would be able to stray from the tried and true meat-seasoned version, but this one wins! Delicious and low fat."

Serving: 4 | Prep: 10 m | Cook: 1 h 7 m | Ready in: 1 h 17 m

Ingredients

- 2 tablespoons olive oil
- 1/2 onion, chopped
- 1 clove garlic, crushed
- 3 cups water
- 1 (16 ounce) package dry black-eyed peas
- 3 tablespoons cider vinegar
- 2 tablespoons white sugar
- 1 teaspoon salt
- 1 dash red pepper flakes, or to taste

Direction

- Heat oil in a large saucepan over medium-high heat. Add onions; sauté until softened and translucent, 5 to 7 minutes. Stir in garlic; cook until fragrant, about 2 minutes. Add water, black-eyed peas, vinegar, sugar, salt, and red pepper flakes. Cook until peas are tender, 60 to 90 minutes.

Nutrition Information

- Calories: 481 calories
- Total Fat: 8.3 g
- Cholesterol: 0 mg
- Sodium: 607 mg
- Total Carbohydrate: 77.5 g
- Protein: 27.1 g

139. Texas Caviar I

"Here's a spicy Texas favorite. Black-eyed peas and black beans are marinated in a fiery, flavorful mixture. This is great with tortilla chips or bread -- and plenty of cold iced tea!"

Serving: 16 | Prep: 15 m | Ready in: 1 h 15 m

Ingredients

- 1/2 onion, chopped
- 1 green bell pepper, chopped
- 1 bunch green onions, chopped
- 2 jalapeno peppers, chopped
- 1 tablespoon minced garlic
- 1 pint cherry tomatoes, quartered
- 1 (8 ounce) bottle zesty Italian dressing
- 1 (15 ounce) can black beans, drained
- 1 (15 ounce) can black-eyed peas, drained
- 1/2 teaspoon ground coriander
- 1 bunch chopped fresh cilantro

Direction

- In a large bowl, mix together onion, green bell pepper, green onions, jalapeno peppers, garlic, cherry tomatoes, zesty Italian dressing, black beans, black-eyed peas and coriander. Cover and chill in the refrigerator approximately 2 hours. Toss with desired amount of fresh cilantro to serve.

Nutrition Information

- Calories: 107 calories
- Total Fat: 5.4 g
- Cholesterol: 0 mg
- Sodium: 415 mg
- Total Carbohydrate: 11.8 g
- Protein: 3.5 g

140. Texas Caviar II

"Here's a simple version of an old spicy Texas favorite made with black-eyed peas and salsa. Serve with tortilla chips."

Serving: 16 | Prep: 5 m | Ready in: 5 m

Ingredients

- 1 (15 ounce) can black-eyed peas, rinsed and drained
- 1/2 (16 ounce) jar picante sauce
- salt to taste

Direction

- In a medium bowl, mix together black-eyed peas, picante sauce and salt. Chill in the refrigerator before serving.

Nutrition Information

- Calories: 22 calories
- Total Fat: 0.2 g
- Cholesterol: 0 mg
- Sodium: 116 mg
- Total Carbohydrate: 3.9 g
- Protein: 1.3 g

141. Three Bean Salad

"Beans are a great source of protein and fiber and have been shown to reduce cholesterol. Combining the great tastes of Red Kidney Beans, Chick Peas and GOYA® Blackeye Peas, along with fresh herbs and GOYA® Extra Virgin Olive Oil will create a side dish that will impress your family and contribute to their health-conscious diet."

Serving: 8 | Prep: 10 m | Ready in: 10 m

Ingredients

- Salad:
- 1 (15.5 ounce) can Goya Blackeye Peas, drained and rinsed
- 1 (15.5 ounce) can Goya Chick Peas, drained and rinsed
- 1 (15.5 ounce) can Goya Red Kidney Beans, drained and rinsed
- 1 medium cucumber, peeled, seeded and chopped
- 1 red bell pepper, seeded and finely chopped
- 2 tablespoons finely chopped fresh cilantro
- Dressing:
- 3 tablespoons Goya Red Wine Vinegar
- 2 packets Goya Salad and Vegetable Seasoning
- 1 tablespoon Goya Lemon Juice
- 1/2 cup Goya Extra Virgin Olive Oil

Direction

- In large serving bowl, mix together black-eyed peas, chick peas, kidney beans, cucumbers, peppers, and cilantro.
- In small bowl, whisk together vinegar, salad, vegetable seasoning and lemon juice. Slowly drizzle in olive oil, whisking

constantly, until blended. Pour dressing over bean mixture. Toss well to coat completely.

142. Toddly Mans Big House BlackEyed Peas

"Hearty. Earthy. Gnarly. Yummy. This is a big recipe and meant to be stirred with joy and shared with many. It is an excuse for you to finally find and patronize an awesome kielbasy maker, and something fun and wonderful to do with the mountains of turkey stock you froze after Thanksgiving.

Make this in a really big pot you inherited from your really big family or borrowed from the Quaker Meeting House. Forget someone important to you at Christmas? No problem! Show up with a container of these black-eyed peas for New Year's, and bring a six-pack of dry hard cider!"

Serving: 30 | Prep: 30 m | Cook: 2 h 10 m | Ready in: 10 h 40 m

Ingredients

- 5 pounds dry black-eyed peas
- 2 pounds smoked turkey wings
- 14 cups turkey stock, or as needed to cover
- 5 stalks celery, diced
- 1 teaspoon red pepper flakes
- 2 cups turkey stock
- 6 onions, diced
- 8 carrots, chopped
- 2 teaspoons ground black pepper
- 3 tablespoons salt
- 1 1/2 tablespoons garlic powder (optional)
- 1 pound smoked garlic kielbasa, diced

Direction

- Fill a large pot with water and soak black-eyed peas overnight. Pour out soaking liquid, cover black-eyed peas with fresh water, and drain. Add turkey wings to black-eyed peas.
- Set pot over medium heat and pour 14 cups turkey stock into peas; bring to a boil. Stir celery and red pepper flakes into peas; reduce heat to low. Simmer for 30 minutes. Remove turkey wings and set aside; chop turkey meat when cool. Pour 2 cups more turkey stock into peas as needed and stir chopped turkey wing meat, onions, and carrots into mixture. Bring back to a simmer and stir black pepper, salt, and garlic powder (if using) into black-eyed peas. Simmer for 1 1/2 more hours.
- Toss diced kielbasa into black-eyed peas, simmer until black-eyed peas and vegetables are tender, about 10 more minutes, and serve.

Nutrition Information

- Calories: 354 calories
- Total Fat: 8.9 g
- Cholesterol: 29 mg
- Sodium: 1536 mg
- Total Carbohydrate: 46.9 g
- Protein: 23.1 g

143. Tutu Dutch Antilles Bean Porridge

"This sweet and savory porridge made of black eyed peas is eaten for dinner."

Serving: 4 | Prep: 15 m | Cook: 45 m | Ready in: 9 h

Ingredients

- 2 cups dried black-eyed peas
- 1 tablespoon vegetable oil
- 1/2 onion, finely chopped
- 3 cloves garlic, minced
- 1 cup all-purpose flour
- 5 cups water
- 2 teaspoons ground nutmeg
- 2 tablespoons white sugar

Direction

- Cover black-eyed peas with water, and soak overnight.
- Heat vegetable oil in a large saucepan over medium heat. Stir in garlic and onion, and cook until softened, about 4 minutes. Stir in flour until evenly combined with onion. Add water, nutmeg, and sugar. Drain peas, and add to saucepan. Bring to a boil over high heat, then reduce heat to medium-low, and simmer until the black-eyed peas are tender, about 30 minutes.

Nutrition Information

- Calories: 256 calories

- Total Fat: 4.6 g
- Cholesterol: 0 mg
- Sodium: 5 mg
- Total Carbohydrate: 47.9 g
- Protein: 5.9 g

144. Vegan Cajun Hoppin John

"This dish is just spicy enough to enhance, rather than take away from, its great depth of flavor. Goes well with cornbread."

Serving: 6 | Prep: 10 m | Cook: 25 m | Ready in: 35 m

Ingredients

- 1 onion, diced
- 1 green bell pepper, diced
- 1 tablespoon canola oil, or as needed
- 3 cups cooked brown rice
- 1 (16 ounce) can red kidney beans, drained
- 10 ounces tomato paste
- 1 (10 ounce) package frozen black-eyed peas
- 15 drops hot sauce (such as Tabasco®)
- 1 pinch smoked salt, or to taste
- 1 pinch dill weed, or to taste
- 1 pinch mustard powder, or to taste
- 1 pinch garlic powder, or to taste
- 1 pinch dried savory, or to taste

Direction

- Combine onion and green bell pepper in a skillet; add enough canola oil to coat onion and bell pepper. Cover skillet and cook onion and bell pepper over medium heat until tender, about 15 minutes.
- Mix rice, kidney beans, tomato paste, black-eyed peas, hot sauce, smoked salt, dill weed, mustard powder, garlic powder,

and savory into onion and bell pepper; cook and stir until heated through, about 10 minutes more.

Nutrition Information

- Calories: 289 calories
- Total Fat: 4.1 g
- Cholesterol: 0 mg
- Sodium: 802 mg
- Total Carbohydrate: 54.5 g
- Protein: 11.3 g

145. Vegetarian Southwest OnePot Dinner

"Easy, delicious slow cooker recipe that uses some of those dry beans hiding in your pantry. Just about any bean can be substituted for the black-eyed peas. If you don't want to soak beans overnight, you can use the canned variety."

Serving: 6 | Cook: 2 h 30 m | Ready in: 2 h 30 m

Ingredients

- 1 1/2 cups dried black-eyed peas, soaked overnight
- 1 green bell pepper, diced
- 1 onion, chopped
- garlic cloves, chopped
- 1 (10 ounce) can sweet corn, drained
- 1 (28 ounce) can diced tomatoes
- 1/4 cup chili powder
- 2 teaspoons ground cumin
- 2 cups cooked rice
- 1/2 cup shredded Cheddar cheese

Direction

- Drain and rinse black-eyed peas thoroughly. Place peas, green pepper, onion, garlic, corn, and tomatoes, in slow cooker. Season with chili powder, and cumin; stir until well blended.
- Cover and cook on high for 2 hours. Stir in rice, and cheese. Continue to cook for a further 30 minutes.

Nutrition Information

- Calories: 342 calories
- Total Fat: 6.2 g
- Cholesterol: 12 mg
- Sodium: 460 mg
- Total Carbohydrate: 59 g
- Protein: 17.3 g

Chapter 3: Fava Beans
***

146. Asturian Beans with Clams

"A typical dish from Asturias, Spain. The best way to eat beans!"

Serving: 6 | Prep: 40 m | Cook: 2 h | Ready in: 10 h 40 m

Ingredients

- 1/2 pound dry fava beans
- cold water, as needed
- 3 tablespoons olive oil
- 1 clove garlic, peeled
- 1 bay leaf
- 1 small onion, peeled
- 3 sprigs fresh parsley
- 1 pinch saffron threads
- 3 tablespoons dry bread crumbs
- 1 pound clams in shells
- 1 pinch salt
- 1/4 teaspoon vinegar
- 3/4 cup water
- salt to taste

Direction

- Place the beans in a large container and cover with several inches of cool water; let stand for 8 hours or overnight. Drain.
- Transfer the beans to a saucepan, cover with cold water, and bring the water just to boiling over high heat.
- Pour the olive oil into a large pot. Add the garlic clove, bay leaf, whole peeled onion, and parsley sprigs. (If you have kitchen

twine, tie the parsley sprigs together so they'll be easier to remove.)
- When the water and beans are boiling, drain the beans and pour them into the pot with the olive oil and seasonings. Add fresh cold water to cover. Cover the pan and cook the beans over very low heat until just tender, about 1 1/2 hours. Remove the onion and parsley sprigs.
- Crush the saffron threads in a mortar and pestle, place into a small bowl, and add a little of the bean-cooking water to soften the threads. Pour the saffron into the beans and mix well. Sprinkle the bread crumbs over the beans, cover the pan, and cook for another 30 minutes or until the beans are very tender.
- Scrub the clams in cold water with a pinch of salt and a few drops of vinegar. While the beans are simmering, transfer the clams to a skillet with 3/4 cup of water or wine (see Cook's Note). Cover the pan and bring the water to a boil, stirring occasionally, until all of the clams have opened. Discard any clams that don't open. Remove the clams from the cooking liquid with a slotted spoon and set aside. Strain the cooking liquid through a cheesecloth-lined strainer to remove any sand and add the liquid to the beans.
- When the beans are tender, add salt to taste and stir in the reserved clams. Ladle the beans and clams into bowls and serve.

Nutrition Information

- Calories: 221 calories
- Total Fat: 7.6 g
- Cholesterol: 6 mg
- Sodium: 64 mg
- Total Carbohydrate: 28.8 g
- Protein: 10.4 g

147. Besara Egyptian Fava Bean Soup

"Ful beans, broad beans, or fava beans, the name depends on your region, pureed into a delicious and hearty soup that is vegan to boot."

Serving: 4 | Prep: 30 m | Cook: 1 h 10 m | Ready in: 9 h 40 m

Ingredients

- 3 cups skinless dried fava beans
- 5 cups water
- 3 tablespoons olive oil
- 2 leek (white part only), chopped
- 1 1/2 onions, chopped
- 5 cloves garlic, chopped
- 1 cup chopped fresh spinach, or to taste
- 1 teaspoon ground cumin, or more to taste
- salt and pepper to taste

Direction

- Place beans in a large pot with water to cover. Soak 8 hours to overnight.
- Drain beans and return to pot with 5 cups fresh water. Bring to a boil and simmer until soft, 45 minutes to 1 hour.
- Heat olive oil in a skillet over medium heat. Add leeks, onions, and garlic; sauté until softened, about 5 minutes. Add to the pot with the beans.
- Add spinach, cumin, salt, and pepper to the soup and cook gently, 15 to 30 minutes more.

- Fill blender halfway with soup. Cover and hold lid down with a potholder; pulse a few times before leaving on to blend. Pour into a pot. Repeat with remaining soup.
- Heat until warm until ready to serve.

Nutrition Information

- Calories: 527 calories
- Total Fat: 12.2 g
- Cholesterol: 0 mg
- Sodium: 84 mg
- Total Carbohydrate: 77.7 g
- Protein: 31.2 g

148. Buddha Bowl Power Menu

"Build up your power menu with this Buddha bowl -- a nutritious meal filled with protein from fava beans, Swiss cheese, egg, peas, and yogurt, plus tons of extras including cinnamon energy bites served with a blueberry drink."

Serving: 1 | Prep: 30 m | Cook: 20 m | Ready in: 9 h 50 m

Ingredients

- Cinnamon Energy Bites:
- 1 cup raw cashews
- 6 dates, pitted
- 1 tablespoon flaxseed meal
- 1/8 teaspoon ground cinnamon
- 1 pinch salt
- 1 tablespoon coconut oil
- Buddha Bowl:
- 1 cup water
- 1/2 cup brown rice
- 1 pinch salt
- 1/2 cup fresh fava beans, shelled
- 1/4 red bell pepper, diced
- 1/4 cup frozen peas
- 1/4 cup diced Swiss cheese
- 1/4 cup canned artichoke hearts, drained and chopped
- 2 teaspoons Dijon mustard
- 2 tablespoons olive oil
- 1 teaspoon white wine vinegar
- 1 hard-boiled egg
- 1/2 cup plain yogurt
- 1/4 avocado, diced
- 2 tablespoons pomegranate seeds

- 1 teaspoon chia seeds
- Blueberry Drink:
- 1/4 cup frozen blueberries
- 2 tablespoons pomegranate seeds
- 3 jasmine flower buds
- 2 cups water

Direction

- Combine cashews, dates, flaxseed meal, cinnamon, and 1 pinch salt in a food processor and blend until very well mixed. Add coconut oil and continue to blend until mixture sticks together. Roll into 20 gumball-sized bites and place on a baking tray. Freeze at least 30 minutes. Store cinnamon energy bites in freezer or refrigerator until ready to serve.
- Bring water, brown rice, and 1 pinch salt to a boil in a saucepan. Reduce heat to medium-low, cover, and simmer for 8 minutes. Add fava beans, red bell pepper, and peas. Cook until rice is tender, about 6 minutes more. Drain if necessary, but do not rinse. Allow to cool completely, about 30 minutes.
- Combine cooled cooked rice, Swiss cheese, and artichoke hearts in a bowl. Mix olive oil, mustard, and white wine vinegar together in a small bowl; pour dressing over rice mixture and toss. Transfer to a bento box with the hard-boiled egg.
- Place yogurt in a separate compartment of the bento box and top with avocado, 2 tablespoons pomegranate seeds, and chia seeds. Add energy bites to another compartment of the bento box. Refrigerate until ready to serve.
- Combine blueberries, 2 tablespoons pomegranate seeds, and jasmine buds in a portable drink container. Add water. Refrigerate 8 hours to overnight. Serve with the bento box.

Nutrition Information

- Calories: 2411 calories
- Total Fat: 136 g
- Cholesterol: 250 mg
- Sodium: 1911 mg
- Total Carbohydrate: 242.3 g
- Protein: 77.4 g

149. Easy Fava Bean Salad

"Just tear off pieces of warm pita bread and scoop up this delicious Middle Eastern salad."

Serving: 2 | Prep: 15 m | Ready in: 15 m

Ingredients

- 1 (14.5 ounce) can fava beans, drained and rinsed
- 1/2 onion, chopped (optional)
- 1/2 tomato, chopped (optional)
- 1 large lemon, juiced
- 3 tablespoons chopped fresh parsley
- 1 tablespoon extra-virgin olive oil
- 1 tablespoon sea salt (optional)
- 1 clove garlic, minced

Direction

- Mash fava beans in a bowl using the back of a spoon or pestle. Add onion, tomato, lemon juice, parsley, olive oil, salt, and garlic; mix well.

Nutrition Information

- Calories: 274 calories
- Total Fat: 7.7 g
- Cholesterol: 0 mg
- Sodium: 3043 mg
- Total Carbohydrate: 41.2 g
- Protein: 10.8 g

150. Easy Mediterranean Pasta

"This fusion dish is quick and easy. It combines some classic ingredients from the lovely Mediterranean region with a Middle Eastern touch. This simple recipe is perfect hot or cold for summer evenings."

Serving: 4 | Prep: 15 m | Cook: 25 m | Ready in: 40 m

Ingredients

- 1 (16 ounce) package penne pasta
- 1 teaspoon olive oil
- 1 teaspoon minced garlic
- 4 roma (plum) tomatoes, diced
- 1 small green bell pepper, diced
- 1 (14.5 ounce) can fava beans, drained
- 1 small onion, diced
- 1/4 cup lemon juice
- 1/2 cup grated halloumi cheese
- 1/4 cup sliced almonds

Direction

- Bring a large pot of lightly salted water to a boil. Add the pasta and return the water to a boil. Stir the olive oil and garlic into the pasta and water; continue cooking until cooked through yet firm to the bite, about 11 minutes; drain. Reduce the heat to medium-low and return the pasta to the pot.
- Stir the tomatoes, bell pepper, fava beans, onion, and lemon juice into the pasta; simmer together until hot and the flavors have melded, 7 to 8 minutes. Top with halloumi cheese and sliced almonds to serve.

Nutrition Information

- Calories: 604 calories
- Total Fat: 10.9 g
- Cholesterol: 11 mg
- Sodium: 363 mg
- Total Carbohydrate: 105.3 g
- Protein: 24.9 g

151. Fava and Butter Bean Salad

"This salad is so delicious, so refreshing, so satisfying, and so easy that you must try it. One key to this simple combination is letting it chill in the fridge for a few hours to marry all the flavors. You can substitute parsley or basil for the mint, but I beg you to try it with the mint. There is something about the taste of fava beans that the mint really brings out like no other herb."

Serving: 4 | Prep: 10 m | Cook: 10 m | Ready in: 1 h 20 m

Ingredients

- 1 1/2 cups shelled fava beans
- 1/2 lemon, juiced, or more to taste
- 1 clove garlic, crushed
- 1 pinch red pepper flakes, or to taste (optional)
- salt and ground black pepper to taste
- 1/4 cup olive oil, divided
- 1 (14 ounce) jar butter beans, rinsed and drained
- 1/2 cup diced roasted red peppers
- 2 tablespoons chopped fresh mint

Direction

- Bring a large pot of lightly salted water to a boil. Add the fava beans and cook until skins are translucent and easy to pull away, about 6 minutes. Transfer beans with a slotted spoon to a bowl of ice water; cool to room temperature, 1 to 2 minutes. Squeeze each bean at one end to remove the bean from its skin; discard skins and reserve beans.
- Whisk lemon juice, garlic, red pepper flakes, salt, and black pepper together in a large bowl; slowly whisk 2 tablespoons

olive oil into lemon juice mixture until dressing is thick and emulsified.
- Stir fava beans, butter beans, roasted red peppers, and mint into dressing; toss to coat beans completely. Drizzle remaining olive oil over the top and season salad with salt and black pepper. Cover and refrigerate until flavors blend, at least 1 hour.

Nutrition Information

- Calories: 393 calories
- Total Fat: 14.6 g
- Cholesterol: 0 mg
- Sodium: 491 mg
- Total Carbohydrate: 47.5 g
- Protein: 19.8 g

152. Fava Bean Dip Foul Mudammas

"A Mediterranean-style dip that is made from fava beans instead of chickpeas. It has a smooth, delicious flavor that will turn any bean dip lover into an instant fan. Can be used as a dip for pita bread, spelt chips, vegetables, or as a sandwich spread."

Serving: 6 | Prep: 10 m | Ready in: 10 m

Ingredients

- 1 (14.5 ounce) can fava beans, drained and rinsed
- 2 tablespoons extra-virgin olive oil
- 1 tablespoon tahini
- 1 tablespoon fresh lemon juice
- 1 large clove garlic, peeled
- 1 teaspoon shoyu (Japanese soy sauce)
- 1 teaspoon brown rice vinegar
- 1/2 teaspoon ginger juice
- 1/2 teaspoon hot chile oil

Direction

- Blend fava beans, olive oil, tahini, lemon juice, garlic, shoyu, brown rice vinegar, ginger juice, and chile oil in a blender on medium speed until smooth, about 5 minutes.

Nutrition Information

- Calories: 118 calories

- Total Fat: 6.4 g
- Cholesterol: 0 mg
- Sodium: 185 mg
- Total Carbohydrate: 11.6 g
- Protein: 3.7 g

153. Fava Bean Hummus with Smoked Trout

"A quick and easy favorite. This recipe features flaky smoked trout, creamy fava bean hummus, and topped with just a touch of tart pickled red onion."

Serving: 20 | Prep: 35 m | Cook: 5 m | Ready in: 40 m

Ingredients

- 1 loaf crusty whole-wheat bread, cut into 1/2-inch slices
- Hummus:
- 2 cups cooked fava beans
- 1/2 cup olive oil
- 1 shallot, finely chopped
- 1 tablespoon lemon juice
- 1 clove garlic, minced
- 1 teaspoon ground cumin
- salt and ground black pepper to taste
- Gribiche Sauce:
- 1 cup mayonnaise
- 2 hard-boiled eggs, peeled and roughly chopped
- 4 cornichons, roughly chopped
- 1/2 cup packed chervil
- 1 tablespoon Dijon mustard
- 1 tablespoon salt-packed capers, rinsed
- 4 ounces smoked trout fillets, skinned
- 1/2 cup pickled red onions

Direction

- Preheat oven to 350 degrees F (175 degrees C). Arrange bread slices on a baking sheet.
- Place fava beans, olive oil, shallot, lemon juice, garlic, and cumin in a food processor. Blend until smooth. Season with salt and pepper.
- Combine mayonnaise, eggs, cornichons, chervil, mustard, and capers in a small food processor. Whip until gribiche sauce is thoroughly combined.
- Bake bread in the preheated oven until lightly toasted, 5 to 7 minutes.
- Top bread with hummus, smoked trout, pickled onions, and the gribiche sauce.

Nutrition Information

- Calories: 228 calories
- Total Fat: 16 g
- Cholesterol: 30 mg
- Sodium: 382 mg
- Total Carbohydrate: 14.9 g
- Protein: 6.8 g

154. Fava Bean Salad

"You can prepare this flavorful fava bean salad made with tomatoes, onion, and cucumber tossed with fresh parsley, lemon juice and olive oil in minutes. Makes a great, simple, side dish for traditional Middle Eastern meals."

Serving: 4 | Prep: 20 m | Ready in: 20 m

Ingredients

- 1 (19 ounce) can fava beans, drained
- 2 medium fresh tomatoes, chopped
- 1 small onion, diced
- 1 cucumber, diced
- 2 cloves garlic, minced
- 1/4 cup chopped fresh parsley
- 1 lemon, juiced
- 3 tablespoons olive oil
- 1 teaspoon ground cumin
- salt and black pepper to taste

Direction

- Combine fava beans, tomatoes, onion, and cucumber in a salad bowl. Toss with garlic, parsley, lemon juice, and olive oil. Season with cumin, and salt and pepper to taste.

Nutrition Information

- Calories: 239 calories
- Total Fat: 11.1 g
- Cholesterol: 0 mg

- Sodium: 555 mg
- Total Carbohydrate: 30.2 g
- Protein: 7.8 g

155. Fava Beans

"This is a delicious and simple Middle Eastern dish that's very easy to make. You can get a can of cooked fava beans in any Middle Eastern store. Serve with pita bread."

Serving: 2 | Prep: 15 m | Cook: 7 m | Ready in: 23 m

Ingredients

- 1 teaspoon vegetable oil
- 1 onion, chopped
- 1 tomato, chopped
- 1 tablespoon tomato paste
- 1 teaspoon water, if needed
- 1 (15 ounce) can fava beans, drained
- 1 tablespoon water
- 1 tablespoon ground cumin
- 1 1/2 teaspoons salt
- 1 1/2 teaspoons ground black pepper
- 1 teaspoon ground red pepper (optional)
- 2 tablespoons olive oil
- 2 tablespoons finely chopped parsley (optional)

Direction

- Heat vegetable oil in a skillet over medium heat; add onion. Cook and stir for 2 minutes. Add chopped tomato and tomato paste; cook until tomatoes are mushy, about 4 minutes. Add 1 teaspoon water, if necessary.
- Pour fava beans into skillet; mash into a paste. Add 1 tablespoon water, cumin, salt, black pepper, and ground red

pepper; stir well. Heat for 1 minute more. Remove from heat; allow to rest for 1 minute. Stir in olive oil and parsley.

Nutrition Information

- Calories: 404 calories
- Total Fat: 17.8 g
- Cholesterol: 0 mg
- Sodium: 2234 mg
- Total Carbohydrate: 50.9 g
- Protein: 13 g

156. Fava Beans in Tahini Sauce

"A delicious recipe I learned from an Egyptian friend. If you don't want a strong garlic taste, feel free to cook the garlic with the onion. You can stuff this mixture into a pita, add a dollop of plain yogurt, and enjoy!"

Serving: 4 | Prep: 10 m | Cook: 15 m | Ready in: 25 m

Ingredients

- 1 tablespoon olive oil
- 1 medium onion, chopped
- 1 (15 ounce) can fava beans, drained
- 1 lemon, juiced
- 1/3 cup tahini
- 5 cloves garlic, crushed
- salt and pepper to taste

Direction

- Heat olive oil in small to medium saucepan over medium-high heat. Cook onion in oil until softened.
- Stir in the beans and lemon juice. Next, stir in the tahini until mixture is thick. Then, add the garlic, and cook for a few minutes more. Season to taste with salt and pepper.

Nutrition Information

- Calories: 242 calories
- Total Fat: 14.3 g
- Cholesterol: 0 mg
- Sodium: 500 mg

- Total Carbohydrate: 22 g
- Protein: 9.7 g

157. Foul Medammes Spicy Fava Bean Dip

"Warm spicy fava bean dip; drizzle with additional olive oil to serve."

Serving: 4 | Prep: 10 m | Cook: 15 m | Ready in: 25 m

Ingredients

- 1 1/2 tablespoons olive oil
- 1 small onion, chopped
- 1 tomato, seeded and chopped
- 3 cloves garlic, chopped
- 1 (15 ounce) can fava beans, drained
- lemon, juiced
- 1/2 teaspoon ground cumin
- 1/4 teaspoon ground turmeric
- 1/3 cup tahini
- salt and ground black pepper to taste

Direction

- Heat olive oil in a saucepan over medium-high heat; sauté onion, tomato, and garlic until softened, about 10 minutes. Stir fava beans, lemon juice, cumin, and turmeric into onion mixture; cook until heated through, 3 to 5 minutes. Stir tahini into fava bean mixture and cook until warmed, 2 to 3 minutes; season with salt and pepper.
- Pour fava bean mixture into a blender no more than half full. Cover and hold lid down; pulse a few times before leaving on to blend. Puree in batches until smooth.

Nutrition Information

- Calories: 271 calories
- Total Fat: 18.1 g
- Cholesterol: 0 mg
- Sodium: 485 mg
- Total Carbohydrate: 22.9 g
- Protein: 10.9 g

158. Fresh Fava Beans with Hibiscus Salt and Mint

"When fava beans are in season and abundant, here's a quick way to prepare and serve them without having to remove the peel. Mint is a natural complement for favas, and subtle floral hibiscus salt is a perfect seasoning. Use leftover cooked favas in composed salads, like salade Nicoise."

Serving: 4 | Prep: 15 m | Cook: 8 m | Ready in: 23 m

Ingredients

- Hibiscus Salt:
- 1 teaspoon dried hibiscus flowers
- 1 teaspoon sea salt
- 2 tablespoons extra-virgin olive oil, divided
- 1 large clove garlic, thinly sliced lengthwise
- 1 pound shelled fava beans, unpeeled
- 1 tablespoon chicken stock
- 1 tablespoon chopped fresh mint

Direction

- Pulse hibiscus flowers in a spice grinder until finely ground. Pour into a small jar; add salt. Shake until blended.
- Heat 2 tablespoons olive oil in a heavy skillet over medium-low heat. Cook garlic slices until sizzling, about 30 seconds. Add fava beans and chicken stock; bring to a simmer over medium heat. Reduce heat to medium-low, cover, and cook until fava bean skins begin to wrinkle, about 6 minutes. Uncover and cook for 1 minute more.

- Transfer fava beans to a serving dish. Discard garlic. Drizzle remaining 1 tablespoon oil over fava beans. Garnish with hibiscus salt and mint.

Nutrition Information

- Calories: 450 calories
- Total Fat: 8.5 g
- Cholesterol: < 1 mg
- Sodium: 465 mg
- Total Carbohydrate: 66.6 g
- Protein: 29.7 g

159. Green Risotto with Fava Beans

"I can't stress enough how much better this is if it is stirred constantly. If one arm gets tired, switch arms. Taste the rice for doneness before serving. Nothing worse than a plate of crunchy risotto. Try it, and you will find it is well worth it!"

Serving: 4 | Prep: 30 m | Cook: 30 m | Ready in: 1 h

Ingredients

- 1/2 pound fresh, unshelled fava beans
- 4 cups chicken broth
- 3 tablespoons butter, divided
- 1 small onion, finely chopped
- 1 cup Arborio rice
- 1/4 cup white wine
- 1/4 cup grated Reggiano Parmesan cheese
- salt to taste

Direction

- Bring a large pot of salted water to a boil. Meanwhile, shell the favas and discard the pods. Boil the favas for 4 minutes, strain and then immediately plunge into ice water. Let cool for 2 minutes then pierce the favas and squeeze them out of their skins. Separate 3/4 of the favas and puree in a food processor.
- In a separate large saucepan bring the broth to a simmer, and keep it hot. Meanwhile, in another large saucepan over medium heat, melt 1.5 tablespoons of the butter and add the onions. Reduce the heat to low and cook for about 5 minutes; do not brown the onions. Add the rice and cook, while stirring, for 2

minutes. Add the wine, increase the heat to medium, and stir constantly. When the wine has been absorbed, add a little of the hot stock. Once the stock is absorbed, add a little more; repeat this process, stirring constantly, until the rice is cooked through.
- To the cooked rice add the pureed favas, the remaining 1.5 tablespoons of butter, the rest of the favas and the cheese. Cook over medium heat, stirring, until the butter and cheese melt and the puree is incorporated evenly. Season with salt.

Nutrition Information

- Calories: 457 calories
- Total Fat: 11.1 g
- Cholesterol: 32 mg
- Sodium: 1414 mg
- Total Carbohydrate: 69.5 g
- Protein: 16.5 g

160. Grilled Fava Beans

"Many people don't know what to do with fava beans, but they are extremely versatile. They shine in salads, pastas, and on pizzas. Here we're grilling whole pods until the skin is charred and the beans inside are just tender."

Serving: 2 | Prep: 10 m | Cook: 10 m | Ready in: 30 m

Ingredients

- 2 pounds whole fava beans in the shell
- 2 tablespoons olive oil, or more as needed
- 2 lemons, divided
- 1 tablespoon kosher salt, divided
- 3 cloves garlic, bruised
- 1 teaspoon red pepper flakes, or more to taste
- 2 tablespoons sliced fresh mint leaves

Direction

- Place whole fava beans in a mixing bowl. Drizzle generously with at least a tablespoon olive oil and the juice of 1 lemon. Sprinkle with half of the kosher salt; add bruised garlic cloves. Toss to coat pods evenly, and occasionally as the grill heats up.
- Grill beans over high heat, about 5 minutes total per side, turning and moving them until they are charred on the outside and the beans inside are soft. Transfer to a serving platter.
- Drizzle with the remaining olive oil; sprinkle with the remaining salt. Add red pepper flakes and mint leaves. Toss to coat. To eat, split open the pod and eat the beans inside, or serve them on half the shell.

Nutrition Information

- Calories: 1679 calories
- Total Fat: 20.7 g
- Cholesterol: 0 mg
- Sodium: 2941 mg
- Total Carbohydrate: 267.1 g
- Protein: 119.1 g

161. Jacys MiddleEastern Fava Bean Stew

"This is called 'Middle-Eastern' fava bean stew and not 'Moroccan' because I have also borrowed flavors from my Lebanese roots. This stew came to me on a Saturday afternoon when we were desperately low on groceries and had no meat in the freezer. The first time my carnivorous partner tried it, he honestly thought it contained meat. I have made this many times, and he devours it with relish! To make this dish completely vegetarian/vegan, omit the anchovies. Serve with steamed basmati rice, couscous or bulgur."

Serving: 6 | Prep: 20 m | Cook: 1 h 45 m | Ready in: 2 h 5 m

Ingredients

- Harissa Paste:
- 1 teaspoon coriander seeds
- 1 teaspoon caraway seeds
- 1/2 teaspoon cumin seeds
- 2 cloves garlic
- 1 pinch coarse sea salt
- 2 tablespoons sweet paprika
- 2 tablespoons dried red pepper flakes
- 2 tablespoons extra-virgin olive oil, or as needed
- 2 tablespoons olive oil
- 1 medium onion, minced
- 2 cloves garlic, minced
- 4 anchovy fillets, chopped (optional)
- 2 cups diced peeled butternut squash
- 2 carrots, chopped
- 1/2 red bell pepper, diced
- 1 cup frozen peas
- 1 pinch salt

- 2 cups vegetable broth
- 2 (14.5 ounce) cans fava beans, drained
- 1 (14 ounce) can canned tomatoes, diced
- 2 tablespoons tomato paste
- 1 bay leaf
- 1 teaspoon brown sugar
- 3 tablespoons pomegranate molasses
- 1 cup chopped fresh flat-leaf parsley
- 1/4 cup chopped fresh mint (optional)

Direction

- To make harissa paste: Heat a dry skillet over high heat and add coriander, caraway and cumin seeds. Shake pan gently until spices become fragrant, about 2 minutes. Remove pan from heat and pour seeds into mortar and grind with pestle to a fine powder. Add garlic, salt, paprika and dried red pepper flakes, mashing and stirring until garlic is incorporated with the spices. Mixture will be dry and crumbly. Add enough of the 2 tablespoons extra-virgin olive oil until you have a thick paste. Use fewer pepper flakes if you prefer less heat. Set aside.
- Pour 2 tablespoons olive oil into a large pot and add minced onions and garlic. Cook slowly over low heat until onions are translucent, about 10 minutes. Push onions aside in the pot, and stir in the anchovies. Cook anchovies until they soften, mashing them with the back of a wooden spoon until they dissolve. Stir together with the onion and garlic mixture.
- Add the butternut squash, carrots, bell pepper, frozen peas and a pinch of salt. Stir and cook over medium heat for about 5 minutes. Pour in the stock. Bring to a simmer and cook for about a minute.
- Stir in the drained fava beans, diced tomatoes, tomato paste, bay leaf and harissa paste (from step 1). Add brown sugar and

pomegranate molasses. Bring back to a simmer, then reduce heat to low and cook uncovered for about 1 1/2 hours. The long, slow cooking time allows the flavors to deepen.
- Just before serving, stir in the chopped parsley. Top with the mint, if you like.

Nutrition Information

- Calories: 315 calories
- Total Fat: 11.4 g
- Cholesterol: 2 mg
- Sodium: 758 mg
- Total Carbohydrate: 45.1 g
- Protein: 11.7 g

162. Jamaican Oxtail with Broad Beans

"This is a traditional Jamaican dish I was taught to cook by my grandmother."

Serving: 4 | Prep: 30 m | Cook: 45 m | Ready in: 1 h 15 m

Ingredients

- 1 pound beef oxtail, cut into pieces
- 1 large onion, chopped
- 1 green onion, thinly sliced
- 2 cloves garlic, minced
- 1 teaspoon minced fresh ginger root
- 1 scotch bonnet chile pepper, chopped
- 2 tablespoons soy sauce
- 1 sprig fresh thyme, chopped
- 1/2 teaspoon salt
- 1 teaspoon black pepper
- 2 tablespoons vegetable oil
- 1 1/2 cups water
- 1 cup canned fava beans, drained
- 1 teaspoon whole allspice berries
- 1 tablespoon cornstarch
- 2 tablespoons water

Direction

- Toss the oxtail with the onion, green onion, garlic, ginger, chile pepper, soy sauce, thyme, salt, and pepper. Heat the vegetable oil in a large skillet over medium-high heat. Brown the oxtail in

the skillet until browned all over, about 10 minutes. Place into a pressure cooker, and pour in 1 1/2 cup water. Cook at pressure for 25 minutes, then remove from heat, and remove the lid according to manufacturer's directions.
- Add the fava beans and allspice berries, and bring to a simmer over medium-high heat. Dissolve the cornstarch in 2 tablespoons water, and stir into the simmering oxtail. Cook and stir a few minutes until the sauce has thickened, and the beans are tender.

Nutrition Information

- Calories: 425 calories
- Total Fat: 22.4 g
- Cholesterol: 125 mg
- Sodium: 1089 mg
- Total Carbohydrate: 17.6 g
- Protein: 38.8 g

163. Lebanese Bean Salad

"Quick, easy, and tasty. Can be used as a side dish or a snack on it's own. Great as a salad topper. Good with sea salt kettle chips, or toast."

Serving: 5 | Prep: 10 m | Ready in: 2 h 10 m

Ingredients

- 1 (15 ounce) can fava beans, drained and rinsed
- 1 (15 ounce) can chickpeas, drained and rinsed
- 1 (15.5 ounce) can white beans, drained and rinsed
- 1/4 cup chopped flat leaf parsley, or more to taste
- 3 tablespoons olive oil
- 2 cloves garlic, minced
- 1 lemon, juiced
- kosher salt and ground black pepper to taste

Direction

- Mix fava beans, chickpeas, white beans, parsley, olive oil, garlic, and lemon juice together in a bowl. Season with kosher salt and black pepper. Chill and marinate in refrigerator for at least 2 hours.

Nutrition Information

- Calories: 312 calories
- Total Fat: 9.3 g
- Cholesterol: 0 mg
- Sodium: 418 mg
- Total Carbohydrate: 44.7 g

- Protein: 13.2 g

164. Meze Fava Beans

"Fava beans sauteed with onions. A traditional Turkish dish. Served at room temperature with garlic yogurt."

Serving: 12 | Prep: 15 m | Cook: 15 m | Ready in: 30 m

Ingredients

- 3 tablespoons olive oil
- 1/2 onion, chopped
- 1 1/2 pounds fresh fava beans, shelled
- 2 tablespoons water
- 1 teaspoon all-purpose flour
- 1 cup boiling water
- 1 teaspoon lemon juice
- 1/2 teaspoon white sugar
- salt to taste
- 1/2 cup chopped fresh dill

Direction

- Heat oil in a skillet over medium heat. Add onions; cook and stir until fragrant, about 1 minute. Toss in fava beans and cook until slightly tender, about 2 minutes.
- Mix 2 tablespoons water and flour together in a bowl; pour into the fava bean mixture. Add 1 cup water, lemon juice, sugar, and salt. Cover and bring to a boil. Reduce heat to low and simmer until fava beans are very tender, about 5 minutes.
- Stir dill into the fava bean mixture; continue simmering until flavors are combined, about 2 minutes. Let cool to room temperature.

Nutrition Information

- Calories: 229 calories
- Total Fat: 4.3 g
- Cholesterol: 0 mg
- Sodium: 22 mg
- Total Carbohydrate: 34.4 g
- Protein: 15 g

165. Middle Eastern Bean Dip Foul Mudammas

"My best friend is Syrian and taught me to make this. It is often eaten for breakfast, but I like to make it for dinner. It is vegan and great for fasting periods. If you cannot find fava beans, check a middle eastern market. Add more lemon juice if you like it bitter! Serve with pita bread. It's also great with Kalamata olives, feta cheese, and lemon wedges.
"

Serving: 4 | Prep: 15 m | Cook: 15 m | Ready in: 30 m

Ingredients

- 2 teaspoons olive oil
- 1 onion, chopped
- 1 (15 ounce) can fava beans, rinsed and drained
- 1 (15 ounce) can garbanzo beans (chickpeas), rinsed and drained
- 1 cup water
- 1/2 (6 ounce) can tomato paste
- 1/2 cup lemon juice
- 1 tablespoon olive oil
- 3 cloves garlic, minced
- 1 tablespoon tahini
- 2 teaspoons ground cumin

Direction

- Heat 2 teaspoons olive oil in a skillet over medium heat; cook and stir the onion in the hot oil until tender, about 5 minutes.

Add the fava beans, garbanzo beans, and water to the onion; bring to a boil, stirring occasionally. Stir the tomato paste, lemon juice, 1 tablespoon olive oil, the garlic, tahini, and cumin through the bean mixture; return the mixture to a boil and allow to cook at a boil for 5 minutes. Remove from heat.
- Pour the mixture into a blender. Hold the lid of the blender in place with a towel and start the blender, using a few quick pulses to get the mixture moving before leaving it on to puree to your desired consistency.

Nutrition Information

- Calories: 290 calories
- Total Fat: 9.3 g
- Cholesterol: 0 mg
- Sodium: 592 mg
- Total Carbohydrate: 43.4 g
- Protein: 10.7 g

166. Pasta with Baby Broccoli and Beans

"Tuscan vegetarian comfort food. Omit the cheese to make it vegan."

Serving: 4 | Prep: 10 m | Cook: 15 m | Ready in: 25 m

Ingredients

- 1 (1 pound) package whole-wheat penne pasta
- 1/4 cup olive oil
- 1/2 whole head garlic, slivered
- 1/2 teaspoon crushed red pepper flakes
- 2 bunches baby broccoli (such as Broccolini®)
- 1 (14.5 ounce) can fava beans, rinsed and drained
- 1/4 cup sun-dried tomatoes
- 2 tablespoons grated Parmesan cheese

Direction

- Bring a large pot of lightly salted water to a boil. Cook the pasta in boiling water until cooked through yet firm to the bite, about 11 minutes; drain.
- While the pasta cooks, heat the olive oil in a skillet over medium heat. Cook the garlic and red pepper flakes in the hot oil briefly, about 1 minutes. Stir the broccolini into the garlic; cook and stir together for 5 minutes. Add the fava beans and sun-dried tomatoes and cook until the beans are completely warmed, 3 to 4 minutes. Remove from heat and toss with the drained pasta in a large bowl. Sprinkle with the Parmesan cheese to serve.

Nutrition Information

- Calories: 736 calories
- Total Fat: 16.8 g
- Cholesterol: 2 mg
- Sodium: 426 mg
- Total Carbohydrate: 113.4 g
- Protein: 35 g

167. Persian Sabzi Polo Herb Rice with Fava Beans

"This is a Persian dish which I often make for my husband. It will taste much better if you use fresh herbs. It also goes very well with either fish or chicken. Hope you like it."

Serving: 16 | Prep: 20 m | Cook: 55 m | Ready in: 1 h 15 m

Ingredients

- 6 cups water
- 4 cups uncooked long-grain white rice
- 3 tablespoons vegetable oil
- 1/2 cup water
- 1 bunch fresh dill, chopped
- 1 bunch fresh parsley, chopped
- 1 bunch fresh cilantro, chopped
- 2 cups fresh or frozen fava beans
- ground turmeric to taste
- ground cinnamon to taste
- 1 teaspoon salt
- 1 teaspoon pepper

Direction

- In a large saucepan bring water to a boil. Rinse rice; stir into boiling water. Boil just until rice rises to the surface of the water. Drain rice and return it to the saucepan. Stir in the oil and water. Mix in the dill, parsley, cilantro, fava beans, turmeric, cinnamon, salt and pepper.
- Cook the rice over medium heat for 5 minutes.

- Reduce heat to the lowest setting. Cover and simmer for 40 to 45 minutes. Note: It's normal to end up with crispy rice (called Tadig) on the bottom of the pot after cooking; it's delicious.

Nutrition Information

- Calories: 234 calories
- Total Fat: 3.1 g
- Cholesterol: 0 mg
- Sodium: 214 mg
- Total Carbohydrate: 44.7 g
- Protein: 5.5 g

168. Portuguese Chourico Beans and Rice

"I grew up on chourico, and this dish is a Portuguese comfort food that my mom always made. I took it upon myself to replicate it with a bit more kick, but even with the changes, it reminds me of being a kid. It's such a warm and satisfying dish."

Serving: 2 | Prep: 10 m | Cook: 30 m | Ready in: 40 m

Ingredients

- 2 cups water
- 1 cup uncooked white rice
- 2 tablespoons olive oil
- 1 dried chourico sausage, halved lengthwise and cut into 1/4-inch slices
- 1/4 Spanish onion, finely chopped
- 3 cloves garlic, minced
- 1 1/2 cups tomato sauce
- 1/2 teaspoon red pepper flakes
- 1 teaspoon Italian seasoning
- salt and pepper to taste
- 1/2 (14.5 ounce) can fava beans, rinsed and drained

Direction

- Bring the water to a boil in a pot; stir the rice into the boiling water, reduce heat to low, place cover on the pot, and allow the rice to cook until all the moisture is absorbed, about 30 minutes.
- As the rice cooks, heat the oil in a skillet over medium heat. Cook the chourico in the hot oil for 2 minutes. Add the onions

and garlic to the sausage and continue cooking until the vegetables are soft and the chourico has browned, 5 to 7 minutes.
- Stir the tomato sauce into the chourico mixture. Reduce heat to low. Season with the red pepper flakes, Italian seasoning, salt, and pepper; simmer until thoroughly heated, 10 to 15 minutes. Stir the fava beans into the mixture and continue cooking just long enough for the beans to heat, 2 to 3 minutes. Serve over rice.

Nutrition Information

- Calories: 722 calories
- Total Fat: 23.7 g
- Cholesterol: 21 mg
- Sodium: 1434 mg
- Total Carbohydrate: 108.6 g
- Protein: 18.6 g

169. Portuguese Fava Bean Stew

"I always loved fava beans stewed Portuguese style. But there is always something missing from the recipes I have. I adjusted the spices and added some chourico, a Portuguese sausage similar to linguica or chorizo. I think this version makes a great dish. Make sure you have plenty of crusty bread for dipping in the sauce!"

Serving: 8 | Prep: 25 m | Cook: 1 h | Ready in: 1 h 25 m

Ingredients

- 2 tablespoons olive oil
- 3 large onions, coarsely chopped
- 2 cloves garlic, minced
- 1 tablespoon chile paste
- 1/4 cup tomato sauce
- 2 cups water
- 3 tablespoons chopped fresh parsley
- salt to taste
- 1/2 teaspoon ground black pepper
- 3 tablespoons paprika
- 1 pound Portuguese chourico sausage, casing removed, sliced 1/4-inch thick
- 2 (19 ounce) cans fava beans, drained

Direction

- Warm the olive oil in a saucepan over medium heat, add the onion and garlic; cook and stir until golden brown. Stir in the chile paste, tomato sauce, water, parsley, salt, pepper, paprika, and sausage.

- Bring the sausage mixture to a boil over high heat; reduce the heat to low and simmer for 40 minutes. Mix in the fava beans and cook 10 minutes for firm beans, or up to 30 minutes for softer beans.

Nutrition Information

- Calories: 365 calories
- Total Fat: 20.9 g
- Cholesterol: 40 mg
- Sodium: 815 mg
- Total Carbohydrate: 30 g
- Protein: 15.3 g

170. Portuguese Favas

"Fava beans with a Portuguese style sauce."

Serving: 8 | Prep: 15 m | Cook: 30 m | Ready in: 45 m

Ingredients

- 5 tablespoons olive oil
- 3 large onions, chopped
- 2 cloves garlic, minced
- 2 tablespoons red pepper flakes
- 1/4 cup tomato sauce
- 2 cups hot water
- 3 tablespoons chopped fresh parsley
- salt to taste
- 1/2 teaspoon black pepper
- 2 teaspoons paprika
- 2 (19 ounce) cans fava beans

Direction

- Heat oil in a large saucepan over medium heat. Sauté onion and garlic until golden brown. Stir in red pepper flakes, tomato sauce, hot water, parsley, salt, pepper and paprika. Bring to a boil, reduce heat and simmer for 30 minutes.
- Gently stir in fava beans. Remove from heat and let stand for several minutes to allow flavors to meld.

Nutrition Information

- Calories: 221 calories
- Total Fat: 9.5 g
- Cholesterol: 0 mg
- Sodium: 300 mg
- Total Carbohydrate: 27.7 g
- Protein: 7.4 g

171. Roasted Kohlrabi Golden Beet and Fava Bean Salad

"Golden beets and kohlrabi are two veggies that call out to me from the produce section whenever they come into season."

Serving: 2 | Prep: 30 m | Cook: 1 h 5 m | Ready in: 2 h 35 m

Ingredients

- 1/2 cup dried brown fava beans
- 3 kohlrabi, peeled and cut into 1-inch cubes
- 3 golden beets, peeled and cut into 1-inch cubes
- salt and pepper to taste
- 1 tablespoon olive oil, or as desired
- salt and pepper to taste
- Vinaigrette:
- 2 tablespoons walnut oil
- 1 tablespoon olive oil
- 1 tablespoon honey-ginger balsamic vinegar
- 1 tablespoon chopped fresh chives
- 1 tablespoon chopped fresh dill
- salt and ground black pepper to taste

Direction

- Put beans in a medium saucepan, cover with water, and bring to a boil. Turn off heat and leave to soak for about 60 minutes.
- Preheat the oven to 375 degrees F (190 degrees C). Line a baking sheet with aluminum foil.

- Combine kohlrabi and beets in a bowl; toss with olive oil and salt. Transfer to the prepared baking sheet.
- Roast kohlrabi and beets in the preheated oven until still firm but not hard when poked with a fork, about 35 minutes. Turn once to avoid burning. Return to the bowl and refrigerate.
- Remove the shells from the softened fava beans using your fingernails. Discard any that can't be shelled. Return beans to the pot and cover with fresh water. Bring to a boil and reduce heat to medium. Cook until tender but not exploded, checking often, 30 to 45 minutes. Drain and add beans to the bowl with the kohlrabi and beets.
- Combine walnut oil, olive oil, balsamic vinegar, chives, dill, salt, and pepper in a small jar with a lid and shake well. Coat the salad with the vinaigrette and season with salt and pepper.

Nutrition Information

- Calories: 507 calories
- Total Fat: 28.2 g
- Cholesterol: 0 mg
- Sodium: 397 mg
- Total Carbohydrate: 53.6 g
- Protein: 17 g

172. Scrumptious Spring Soup

"This recipe goes back to the 16th century and if it's been around for so long, it must be good. Actually, it's more than that, it's awesomely good! The soup is made with a variety of fresh spring produce and ground veal. If you can't find the fresh ingredients or don't feel like shucking peas you can use them frozen. If you want to make a vegetarian dish, omit the veal and pancetta and replace the meat broth with a vegetable broth."

Serving: 8 | Prep: 20 m | Cook: 40 m | Ready in: 1 h

Ingredients

- 2 quarts beef broth
- 1 tablespoon olive oil
- 2 cups minced green onions
- 5 ounces pancetta, minced
- 1/2 pound ground veal
- 2 cups frozen artichoke hearts, thawed
- 2 cups peas
- 2 cups shelled fava beans
- 2 cups sliced fresh asparagus
- 1 1/2 teaspoons salt
- 8 slices day-old crusty bread, cut into 1-inch cubes
- 7 sprigs fresh thyme, leaves stripped
- 2 cloves garlic, crushed
- 1/2 cup olive oil
- 1/2 teaspoon salt
- ground black pepper to taste
- 13 sprigs fresh thyme, leaves stripped
- 1/2 cup grated Parmesan cheese
- 1/4 cup extra-virgin olive oil

Direction

- Preheat an oven to 425 degrees F (220 degrees C). Bring beef broth to a boil in a saucepan over medium-high heat, then reduce heat to medium-low and keep hot.
- Heat 1 tablespoon olive oil in a large pot over medium heat. Cook and stir the green onion until tender, and stir in the pancetta. Cook and stir until the pancetta is browned, then increase heat to medium-high heat and stir in the ground veal. Cook and stir until the veal is crumbly, evenly browned, and no longer pink. Drain and discard any excess grease. Stir in the artichoke hearts, and cook for 1 minute. Stir in the peas, fava beans, and asparagus. Season with 1 1/2 teaspoons salt. Pour in the hot beef broth, and allow soup to simmer until the vegetables are tender and cooked through, 7 to 10 minutes.
- Meanwhile, toss the slices of bread with leaves from 7 sprigs of thyme, garlic, 1/2 cup olive oil, 1/2 teaspoon salt, and pepper. Place bread on a baking sheet.
- Toast in the preheated oven until golden brown, about 10 minutes. Set aside.
- Stir the leaves of 13 sprigs of thyme into the soup, and season with pepper. Serve hot soup in bowls topped with croutons, Parmesan cheese, and a drizzle of extra-virgin olive oil.

Nutrition Information

- Calories: 556 calories
- Total Fat: 29.7 g
- Cholesterol: 30 mg
- Sodium: 1834 mg
- Total Carbohydrate: 48.1 g
- Protein: 27.1 g

173. Swordfish Calabrian Style

"This is a typical dish of southern Italy. Swordfish is marinated in a lemon and oil mixture, then fried and cooked with fava (broad) beans and white wine."

Serving: 4 | Prep: 10 m | Cook: 15 m | Ready in: 25 m

Ingredients

- 3 tablespoons olive oil, divided
- 1 tablespoon fresh lemon juice
- salt and pepper to taste
- 1 1/4 pounds fresh swordfish, cut into chunks
- 1 small onion, chopped
- 1 teaspoon all-purpose flour
- 1 1/2 cups dry white wine
- 1 (19 ounce) can fava beans, drained
- 1 bunch fresh parsley, chopped

Direction

- In a medium bowl, mix together 2 tablespoons of the olive oil, lemon juice, salt and pepper. Add the fish and stir enough to get it coated. Let it marinate for about 15 minutes. Remove fish from the marinade, and pat dry.
- Heat the remaining olive oil in a large skillet over medium-high heat. Fry the onion until golden, then add the fish. Brown the chunks of fish on all sides, then remove from the pan, and set aside.
- Stir the flour into the skillet; cook and stir until lightly browned. Gradually stir in the white wine. Return the fish to the pan, and add the fava beans. Sprinkle with fresh parsley, cover, and

simmer for 2 to 3 minutes, or until the fish flakes easily with a fork. Serve hot.

Nutrition Information

- Calories: 453 calories
- Total Fat: 18.7 g
- Cholesterol: 53 mg
- Sodium: 402 mg
- Total Carbohydrate: 26.3 g
- Protein: 28 g

174. Taameya Egyptian Falafel

"Falafel, or ta'ameya as we call it in Egypt, is an all-time favorite street food. In most parts of the Middle East, falafel is made with ground chickpeas. However, in Egypt, we make it with dried fava beans. They are best served with pita bread, tomato, onions, and tahini sauce."

Serving: 10 | Prep: 20 m | Cook: 8 m | Ready in: 8 h 28 m

Ingredients

- 2 cups dried split fava beans
- 1 red onion, quartered
- 1/2 cup fresh parsley
- 1/2 cup fresh cilantro
- 1/2 cup fresh dill
- 3 cloves garlic
- 1 1/2 teaspoons ground coriander
- 1 1/2 teaspoons salt
- 1 teaspoon ground cumin
- 1 cup sesame seeds (optional)
- vegetable oil for frying

Direction

- Place fava beans in large bowl and cover with several inches of water. Let soak, 8 hours to overnight. Drain.
- Combine soaked fava beans, red onion, parsley, cilantro, dill, garlic, coriander, salt, and cumin in a food processor; process to a dough-like consistency.
- Heat a skillet over medium heat. Add sesame seeds; cook, stirring occasionally, until toasted, about 5 minutes. Transfer to

a large plate.
- Shape fava bean mixture into balls. Roll in sesame seeds to coat.
- Fill a large saucepan 1/4 full with oil; heat over medium heat. Fry fava bean balls in batches until golden brown, 3 to 5 minutes. Drain on paper towels.

Nutrition Information

- Calories: 234 calories
- Total Fat: 12.2 g
- Cholesterol: 0 mg
- Sodium: 359 mg
- Total Carbohydrate: 22.8 g
- Protein: 10.8 g

175. Tuscan Fava Bean and Orecchiette Pasta Salad

"We really love the texture, hardiness and earthiness of the fava beans, however, butter beans or large lima beans may be substituted."

Serving: 2 | Prep: 30 m | Cook: 15 m | Ready in: 1 h 45 m

Ingredients

- 1 cup orecchiette pasta
- Dressing:
- 1/4 cup extra-virgin olive oil
- 3 tablespoons red wine vinegar
- 4 cloves garlic, minced
- 1 teaspoon ground dried thyme
- 1 teaspoon ground black pepper, or to taste
- 1/4 teaspoon salt
- Salad:
- 1 (19 ounce) can fava beans, drained
- 1 cup halved grape tomatoes
- 2/3 cup chopped red onion
- 1/2 cup chopped celery
- 1/4 cup chopped fresh basil

Direction

- Bring a large pot of lightly salted water to a boil. Stir in orecchiette pasta and cook uncovered, stirring occasionally, until tender yet firm to the bite, about 10 minutes. Drain and rinse in cold water.

- Whisk the olive oil, vinegar, garlic, thyme, black pepper, and salt together in a bowl until dressing is mixed.
- Combine the fava beans, cooked pasta, grape tomatoes, red onion, celery, and basil in a large bowl. Toss to coat with the dressing. Cover and chill at least 1 hour.

Nutrition Information

- Calories: 691 calories
- Total Fat: 30.3 g
- Cholesterol: 0 mg
- Sodium: 837 mg
- Total Carbohydrate: 86 g
- Protein: 19.7 g

176. Vegan Fava Bean Salad

"So I had some vegan friends over for a late night soiree and had to get a little creative with what I had. This simple, healthy salad was a hit."

Serving: 4 | Prep: 20 m | Ready in: 1 h 20 m

Ingredients

- 1/2 lemon, juiced
- 2 tablespoons balsamic vinegar
- 1 teaspoon maple syrup
- 1 clove garlic, minced
- 1/3 cup extra virgin olive oil
- 1 cucumber, diced
- 1 small sweet onion, diced
- 2 roma (plum) tomatoes, chopped
- 2 (15 ounce) cans fava beans, drained

Direction

- Whisk the lemon juice, balsamic vinegar, maple syrup, garlic, and olive oil together in a bowl to make the dressing.
- Toss the cucumber, onion, tomatoes, and fava beans together in a large bowl; pour the dressing over the vegetable mixture and toss to coat. Chill for 1 hour before serving.

Nutrition Information

- Calories: 384 calories
- Total Fat: 19.7 g
- Cholesterol: 0 mg

- Sodium: 416 mg
- Total Carbohydrate: 42.2 g
- Protein: 11 g

177. Vegetarian Pumpkin Spinach Chili

"This easy chili is unique and delicious. It has the added bonuses of iron, vitamin A, and protein. It's also completely vegetarian!"

Serving: 9 | Prep: 25 m | Cook: 3 h 20 m | Ready in: 3 h 45 m

Ingredients

- 1 (28 ounce) can diced tomatoes
- 1 (14 ounce) can 100% pure pumpkin
- 1 cup vegetable juice
- 1 cup chopped okra
- 1 cup chopped broccoli
- 1 carrot, peeled and chopped
- 1 small zucchini, diced
- 1 small onion, diced
- 2 tablespoons pumpkin pie spice
- 2 tablespoons white sugar
- 2 tablespoons white vinegar
- 1 teaspoon chili powder, or to taste
- 1 teaspoon salt
- 1/2 teaspoon ground black pepper
- 1 (12 ounce) package vegetarian ground beef crumbles
- 1 (19 ounce) can fava beans, drained
- 2 cups chopped spinach

Direction

- Combine the tomatoes, pumpkin, vegetable juice, okra, broccoli, carrot, zucchini, onion, pumpkin pie spice, sugar, vinegar, chili powder, salt, and pepper in a slow cooker; cook on High until the vegetables are tender, 3 to 4 hours.
- Stir the vegetarian ground beef crumbles, fava beans, and spinach into the tomato mixture; continue cooking until completely warmed, 20 to 30 minutes more.

Nutrition Information

- Calories: 177 calories
- Total Fat: 2.4 g
- Cholesterol: 0 mg
- Sodium: 854 mg
- Total Carbohydrate: 27.1 g
- Protein: 12.1 g

Printed in Great Britain
by Amazon